Personal networking

Personal Networking

How to make your connections count

Mick Cope

An imprint of Pearson Education

London • New York • Toronto • Sydney
Tokyo • Singapore • Hong Kong • Cape Town • New Delhi
Madrid • Paris • Amsterdam • Munich • Milan • Stockholm

PEARSON EDUCATION LIMITED

Head Office:
Edinburgh Gate
Harlow CM20 2JE
Tel: +44 (0)1279 623623
Fax: +44 (0)1279 431059

London Office:
128 Long Acre
London WC2E 9AN
Tel: +44 (0)20 7447 2000
Fax: +44 (0)20 7447 2170
Website: www.business-minds.com

First published in Great Britain in 2003

© Pearson Education Limited 2003

The right of Mick Cope to be identified as Author of this Work has been asserted by him in accordance with the Copyright, Designs and Patents Act 1988.

ISBN 0 273 66359 3

British Library Cataloguing in Publication Data
A CIP catalogue record for this book can be obtained from the British Library.

10 9 8 7 6 5 4 3 2 1

Typeset by Northern Phototypesetting Co. Ltd, Bolton
Printed and bound in Great Britain by Bell & Bain Ltd, Glasgow

The Publishers' policy is to use paper manufactured from sustainable forests.

For Lin, Michael, Joe and Lucy – you
make it all worthwhile – thanks

Contents

Mick Cope books ix
Preface xi
Thanks xiii

1   **Introduction** 1
The need to network 5
Professional networking 7
Paying the net-tax 8

2   **Social capital** 11
Social organization 12
Social capitalization 13
Social capital investment process 14
Social cost 19
Social corruption 20

3   **Network frame** 23
Networking elements 24

4   **Activate abundance** 29
Self abundance 30
Sow before you reap 32
Level of abundance 33
Love the one you're with? 38
Slingshot – use your net's net 41
In summary 44

5   **Build bridges** 47
See their world 47
Knowing you – selling me 57
See the shadows 60
Listen to the language 64
Be like-*able* 68
In summary 72

6 Chart the connections 75
Tie strength 76
Similarity 79
Relational value 82
Network connection chart 85
Network abundance 90
In summary 94

7 Dare to be different 97
You and you alone 98
Bang the symbol 105
Find it – don't fake it 107
Simply simple 108
Sell yourself 109
In summary 111

8 Entrust others 115
Why *entrust* rather than *trust*? 115
Rights and responsibilities 116
Pressing the flesh and kissing babies 117
The trust choice 119
Trust funds 122
Transferable trust 127
Give to get – reciprocity 130
In summary 137

9 Fuel the flow 139
Riding the network S-curve 140
A common tragedy 144
Manage the memes 149
Organization and disorganization 151
Knowledge socialization 154
In summary 158

10 Network management 161

Epilogue 167
Notes 169
Appendix: Network frame 171

Mick Cope books

Leading the Organisation to Learn

Know Your Value? – *Value what you know*

Float-you – *How to capitalize on your talent*

Seven Cs of Consulting

Lead Yourself – Be where others will follow

Personal Networking – *How to make your connections count*

Collaborative Coaching

Preface

Networking is really quite simple – you know someone, who knows someone else, and by virtue of your connection you get tickets for the cup match, rock concert or other big event. This added value comes from your ability to make the most of existing connections and importantly create new connections in areas where you might want to exert influence in the future.

By using your personal network you can enlist others to share your brand with their connections and you can share their brand with your contacts. When all works well, the social capital created across your network can exceed the sum of the parts. This is the emergence of compound value simply because people have taken a selfless approach to helping themselves and others. You grow, your team grows, the company grows and society grows because the collective talent of its people is being optimized.

However, a word of caution. Some personal development books will give you ideas and techniques that offer instantaneous payback. Networking is a very different option. Most of the payback from investment in a professional network comes in the long run. You have to build it before you can use it. You can't really snap your fingers and make a network appear overnight. You will need to invest hour after hour, talking to people on the phone; spend days and days drinking cups of coffee and discussing their issues; and you will have to spend months and months refuelling the contacts as they run out of energy. However, I believe that this investment, when carefully managed, is one of the most important choices you can make to help create sustainable personal success.

> People who optimize their personal capital can change their world. People who optimize their social capital can change the world.

People who optimize their personal capital can change their world. People who optimize their social capital can change the world.

Good luck and drop me a line to let me know how it goes.

Mick
Mick@wizoz.co.uk
www.wizoz.co.uk

Thanks

To those people who have contributed their personal thoughts on networking: Ann Mcnulty, Angela Eden, Anton Fishman, Angela Abell, Brenda Massey, Donald Hudd, Deborah Rowland, Elisabeth Merrick, Fiona Anderson, G. Matthew Bulley, Kenny Whitson, Leo Borwick, Miranda Dodd, Mike Moirr, Simon Masterton, Trevor Waldock, Roland Stainton-Williamson, Victor Newman, Tony Marks.

To those people who have infuenced many of my thoughts on the ideas in this book: Gary Denyer from Bairstow Eves in Rayleigh who is a master at building social relationships. Owen Wilson for his insightful ideas on the benefits of social capital. Also to Stacey Copping and Katie Jackson for being so great. Thanks to Jamie Osler for being so inspirational, and to Mike and Dave from GB Domestics for their help. Also to Peter Campbell for starting my thoughts about the idea of networking. Special thanks to Rachael Stock, Elizabeth Wilson, Rachel Russell and all at Pearson Education for their support and guidance.

'One huge hurdle for me was how to accept the idea of networking. It was first put across to me as an "essential" for corporate success at a management training course. Whether or not I misunderstood, or the way it was put across, I went away with the idea that you built a professional network of "people who might be useful to you", i.e. may at some point further your career. I was horrified at this, it didn't sit easily with my "deeper values" and I guess I rejected it. Now, 10 years later I have rediscovered "networking" but through a more natural process of "we've each got interests in this area – let's see what we might share and help each other".'

Ann McNulty

Introduction

Look in any management book and you will generally find a section that describes a managerial ratio called the *span of control*. This describes the number of people who report to a manager in a hierarchically structured organization. Although its primary purpose is to aid the design of the organization, at a deeper level it is often used as a subtle political power tool. Just listen to how often people use the ratio as a way to indicate their personal power within the organization (I have xxx people under my control).

Figure 1.1   Span of control

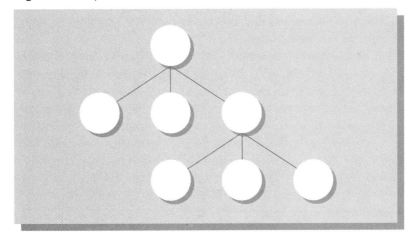

Although it is important to use the span of control as a tool to design traditional organizations, as an indicator of power it is possibly past its time. In the agricultural and industrial era, the whole notion of effective management was about incubating dependence, fostering a strong tie between employee and employer that would stand the test of time and resist everything the market could throw at it. We now exist in an era

> Although it is important to use the span of control as a tool to design traditional organizations, as an indicator of power it is possibly past its time.

that is driven by transitory organizations, flatter structures, a withdrawal of traditional support systems (pensions, health, etc.) and a growing sense of autonomy by the workers as they seek more self-control. As a result, we are moving from an era of dependence to an era of interdependence, where the notion of effectiveness is derived from ability to 'work with' rather than 'work for'.

Geoff Mulgan describes this shift using an old English word of 'connexity', which derives from the Latin *connectere*, to tie or join together. It offers a reminder that the world needs to be measured less by the size of things but more by the connectors that tie the things together. For example, consider the four equations below.

$$2 + 2 =$$
$$2 - 2 =$$
$$2 \times 2 =$$
$$2 \div 2 =$$

The things stay the same but it is the connectors that make the difference. Traditionally people have focused on managing 'things', but now we need to understand how to manage the connectors and in doing this learn how to make the connections count.

As people make their connections count so they begin to unshackle themselves from the chains of corporate slavery. As they learn to bypass the corporate control system and bond with friends, colleagues and classmates, people realize they have the freedom to choose. In the same way that the wheel gave mankind the freedom of mobility, the ability to create wideband connections offers mankind the freedom of choice: the power to change careers without having to get company consent, and the power to create a 'brand new you' without having to get the bosses' approval. This comes because people have bypassed the formal span of control and instead manage through their connections.

The old clichés are often the best, and who you know generally does count for more than what you know. This is not to discount the value of personal knowledge as the primary capital base. But no matter how clever you are, at some point success will be dependent on your ability to access and gain support from the 'right' people.

Successful people do two things. First, they develop a wide span of connections across areas where they wish to exert influence. Second they know

Figure 1.2 Span of connection

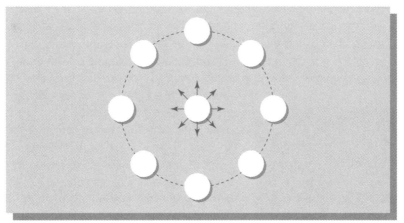

how to make these connections count. It is the two key issues of network construction and leverage that are considered in this book.

As your connections grow and you make these connections count, certain benefits will be accrued:

- **Offer rapid access to resource when you most need it**. This is true in so many cases, from the simple example where you run out of an ink jet cartridge on a Sunday night and you urgently need it for a presentation the following day, to the critical situation where you are desperately trying to get some information about a client but the shutters are up. So you talk to a colleague who knows someone who works for him/her and you manage to get hold of the information.

- **Create a low-cost way to access new people and markets**. Imagine that you work in one department and suddenly hear that a new office is being opened overseas. You are really keen to find out more about a placement and meet the nominated MD but you don't have any way to get close to the situation. By tapping into your network you find someone who is looking after the accommodation build for the office and can give you all the background that you need, as well as help you talk with the new MD.

> Successful people do two things. First, they develop a wide span of connections across areas where they wish to exert influence. Second, they know how to make these connections count.

- **Enhance your market appeal**. The person who knows the right people will always be attractive to others. Think about those people you go to when there is a problem in the office or when you need to find out some political information. Their attractiveness to the market has real brand significance and ensures that both peers and managers value them. The reality is that when the next downsizing comes, this can offer protection against the rampant boss when he realizes that losing you means losing your contacts. Or, when the next growth phase is entered, the director recognizes that your ability to transcend organizational boundaries will enhance the operational capability of her team and so supports your promotion to the senior team. The capability to network has real market value – the trick is to help others understand your capability to make connections count.

> The strength of a wideband professional network is that it gives access to deep and tacit knowledge across a range of areas that you could never hope to touch, understand or gain access to.

■ **Offer advance warning of market disruption**. By having tentacles and connections 'out there' in the places where you don't normally operate, it becomes easier to see if an ill wind is blowing your way. In many ways this is the duty performed by government embassies placed around the world. Although part of their responsibility is to act as a local base station to help people when travelling, there is also an important function to act as a remote sensor to gauge what is happening on the outpost and report back to the home government. In the same way, your network nodes can become your ambassadors.

■ **Rich variety**. One person can have only so much knowledge and wisdom. You may be the brightest bean in the beanbag but at the end of the day there will be things that you don't know. Although access to information is not really a problem in the current era, understanding what that information means in a particular context will not be so readily available as much of it is routed in tacit understanding. The strength of a wideband professional network is that it gives access to deep and tacit knowledge across a range of areas that you could never hope to touch, understand or gain access to.

■ **Learning community**. In many cases the things you need to learn most to do your job are the things that are most difficult to find. When you have just been promoted and need to learn a whole bunch of skills, where do you get them? There might be a course that purports to give you this new-found wisdom, but in most cases it will only skim the surface of the things you really need to know. Much of what you learn when making the jump from team member to team leader, supervisor to office manager, or middle manager to director comes from associating with the right people: people who understand what really goes on and what makes the organization tick. These are the people to network with and they are the people you need to develop a successful relationship with. These people are so crucial to you career development that it is almost impossible to put a hard value on the intangible insight they can offer.

■ **Provide a support network**. At some point in the next month you may well get low about something at work. This might be the failed client bid or a roasting from your boss. Either way, simply having someone to turn to when things get tough has immense value. Never underestimate the value that a close community can offer in the form of a support network.

The whole process of networking rests on a set of deep, complex and often undiscussible human thoughts, feelings and behaviours. For example, you know someone, who knows someone else, and by virtue of your connection you are able to get seats for the new West End show. However, the person you know only came into your network recently, but was willing to help you because you were kind enough to drop him at the airport when his car broke down. However, what wasn't mentioned is that he realized that your company imports children's toys from the Far East and his brother plans to open a market stall selling electronic toys, so he is keen to keep in contact with you as a possible source for the stock. This is a simple process of you scratch my back and I scratch yours.

Wayne Baker nicely sums up what is happening in this situation when he considers the idea of *social capital*. He defines this as the resources that you have access to through your network. These resources include information, ideas, leads, business opportunities, financial capital, power and influence, emotional support, even goodwill, trust and cooperation.[1]

The need to network

Society is changing: the world is being networked through the Web; industry is becoming networked through increasingly complex alliances and partnership; organizations are becoming networked through remote technology; teams are becoming networked as they become more virtual and dispersed in nature; hence, you need to learn how to network more effectively.

Much of this change is being driven by a deeper shift in society and the workplace, namely, changes in the profile of the workforce, a power shift in ownership of the means of production, and greater levels of personal responsibility being given to people (even if they don't want it). With redundancy becoming the norm, the erosion of company security and a general elimination of organizational layers, the lifecycle for jobs and skills is shortening. People will increasingly rotate through different jobs, and as such will need the capability to find new jobs and careers using personal contacts rather than relying on the formal recruitment processes. Already up to 70% of the people who join relocation companies after leaving their company find a new placement through personal contacts rather than the formal employment processes.

> Already up to 70% of the people who join relocation companies after leaving their company find a new placement through personal contacts rather than the formal employment processes.

Although this is important for individuals to understand, it is also important for organizations to learn how to optimize the social capital that provides much of the talent and value within the business. The time when one person can know all the important things within an organization are pretty well over. The smart organization understands that human capital can only be fully optimized if people belong to networks where they can coordinate and amplify their necessarily limited knowledge.[2] This is because the important intellectual capital often sits between people. It is the '+' in the '2 + 2 =' equation. It might not be that one person has the answer to a market problem, rather it is the nature of the soft relationship between the sales, engineering and design department that offers the market differentiator. Thus knowledge is contained in the internal network rather than the banks and banks of company databases.

We can also take a more global view about the importance of networking and the creation of social capital. If you look at the World Bank Poverty Net website (http://www.worldbank.org/poverty/scapital/), it defines social capital as the institutions, relationships, and norms that shape the quality and quantity of a society's social interactions. The argument is that the density of social networks and institutions, and the nature of interpersonal interactions that underlie them, significantly affect the efficiency and sustainability of development programmes. Social cohesion is critical for societies to prosper economically and for development to be sustainable.

The suggestion is that the generation of social capital is a powerful force which helps in a wide range of global dilemmas:

- Crime/violence: shared values and norms can reduce or keep low the level of community violence. People who have informal relations with their neighbours can look out for each other and 'police' their neighbourhoods.

- Economics and trade: there is increasing evidence that trade at the macro level is influenced by social capital – a common property resource whose value depends on the level of interaction between people.

- Education: considerable evidence shows that family, community and state involvement in education improves outcomes.

- Environment: 'common property resource management entails cooperation with a view to ensure the sustainability of resources for the benefit of all community members, in the present and in the future.'

- Poverty and economic development: development and growth specialists are uncovering the importance of social cohesion for societies to prosper economically and for development to be sustainable.

- Rural development: social capital is significant because it affects rural people's capacity to organize for development. Social capital helps groups to perform key development tasks effectively and efficiently.

- Water supply and sanitation: social capital contributes to the sharing of information about sanitation as well as the building of community infrastructure.

This list is by no means exhaustive but what it hopefully indicates is that the notion of networking to create social capital is a bigger and more important issue than is often considered. Our ability to gather and leverage connections is an important one which we all need to understand and deploy carefully.

Professional networking

By professional networking I mean a set of close contacts or associates who will help deliver my value to market. For the musician, it is contacts in the recording, promotion or publishing world; for the house painter, it is shop-keepers who meet potential customers or contract managers in corporate business; for the office manager, it might be people who understand how the financial systems operate. The key thing is that these are people who will 'help' you in the market, THEY ARE NOT THE MARKET. Sorry for the full-on letters, but my definition of a network is 'people who will help amplify my

> The trouble is that so many people see networking as an unethical and unnatural process. They think that making use of personal contacts smacks of Machiavellian abuse and is duplicitous and dishonourable. I would argue that networking is a natural, ethical and enjoyable process, one that we should be encouraged to use from the moment we are born.

personal capital in the market', not a bunch of friends and colleagues to whom I try to sell under the guise of giving them a great opportunity. Active management of these people is *not* networking; it is client relationship management, a whole different ball game and one deliberately not covered in this book.

What I do try to cover is the idea of ethical networking. Let me stress, this is not about you learning to put on a false front, cheesy grin or flash tie: that's not networking – that's plastic sales. Natural networking is about being yourself and using the essence of who you are and your personal capital to build long-term successful and sustainable relationships with other people.

The trouble is that so many people see networking as an unethical and unnatural process. They think that making use of personal contacts smacks of Machiavellian abuse and is duplicitous and dishonourable. I would argue that networking is a natural, ethical and enjoyable process, one that we should be encouraged to use from the moment we are born. The unethical part is when this is done in the shadows and for purely selfish reasons. Then networking is a dangerous corruptive practice that will ultimately destroy the potential value embedded within a relationship.

Part of the reason for writing this book comes from a desire to raise to the surface many of the shadow strategies that people use but don't always admit to. They will talk about their contacts and network over coffee and in the bar on a Friday night, but heaven forbid that it should ever be discussed in an open forum as part of a personal development plan. I hope that by making these ideas available we can start to discuss and understand how we network and from this learn how to improve our capability to transform personal capital into social capital.

Paying the net-tax

Just imagine the last outdoor concert you went to – were there any toilet rolls left in the portables? Unlikely, as I recently learned at great (and embarrassing) cost. Maybe the time to think about toilet rolls is before and not at the concert. In the same way, you cannot just conjure up a network when you need it. The time to think about your network is probably up to two or three years before you are likely to need it. And maybe this is a conservative estimate. If you are looking to make a serious life or career change, then the process of building a robust and sustainable support community might even take up to four or five years.

The development of such a robust network costs, and the primary cost is time. In the same way that you set aside time each month to maintain the house, update your financial records or attend an evening class, so you will need to do the same to build a robust network. It is almost like a self-imposed taxation or savings scheme, where you make regular deposits into a social capital fund in anticipation that you can make withdrawals at a later date. This can be just as difficult and painful as saving for a new car or holiday because so much is being given up for such little apparent short-term return. However, it is the choice to self-impose a net-tax that will deliver benefits in the long run.

> If you meet someone always try to do him or her a kindness or favour without demanding anything in return. This means that you can rest easy at night because people (hopefully) are not viewing you as selfish and manipulative.

If you are serious about building a value-added social network for tomorrow, then you must live it today by making constant emotional deposits with people. If you meet someone always try to do him or her a kindness or favour without demanding anything in return. This means that you can rest easy at night because people (hopefully) are not viewing you as selfish and manipulative. In addition, others might adopt your trait and pay forward with people they network with; the result is that the social capital of your net and your net's net accumulates on a compound basis.

'I have enormous curiosity and interest in other people. Sometimes it connects into a network, sometimes it fizzles out. Whatever the outcome, I find it fascinating.'

Angela Eden

Social capital

One of the most important choices we ever make in life is who to spend time with. As I watched my children grow it became clear on a daily basis how their thoughts, feelings and behaviours were being influenced and shaped by the people they were choosing to spend time with: the sports that Joe chose to play because he spent time with certain people at school, Lucy's first forays in the world of dancing as she started to dance with Stacy and Katie, or PC games that Michael found after talking with people on the Internet.

In the same way that I occasionally felt duty bound to intervene in the children's life to manage their social capital, I have to make conscious choices about the management of my social capital. Do I choose to spend time with a colleague like Carmel who is a social activist and will always help me think deeply through many of my existing beliefs and behaviours, or do I choose to spend time with Gary to develop ideas and themes for future books? Neither is right nor wrong, but that allocation of two hours of my time might seriously affect the next three months of my life and as a result have an impact on my professional career.

> The choice you make about whom to spend time with today can have a dramatic impact on what you do for the rest of your life.

Just think about the five key people in your network and the extent to which your social capital with them enhances your personal capital. Which of them augments it? Do any of them lower its value? Who do you need to spend time with in the next month to achieve your next goal? The choice you make about whom to spend time with today can have a dramatic impact on what you do for the rest of your life.

Social organization

In a perfect world we might like to think that the process of organizing our social life is ordered and under control. However, so often it can be seen to resemble the chaotic interactions that take place in a school playground.

Think about your first day at a new school. In the classroom everything was quite safe because the teacher (hopefully) exercised control over the group and managed the interactions around a set of formalized rules and procedures. Because of that everyone had a chance to speak, and peer engagement was carefully managed. So far so good; you were able to speak to a few classmates in team exercises and made some initial links with people.

Then on the dot of 10.30, the bell rings for a break. Once in the playground all the established rules and procedures are discarded and a new set of regulations comes into play! In the playground the person with the most social capital tends to win. Just walk by any playground and you will see discrete clusters of children playing together. Watch this for a while and the key hub in each cluster will start to stand out. This is the person who has the most influence and has learned to acquire and mobilize his/her social capital most effectively.

In this situation you are on your own – there is no guiding hand of the teacher to help out. For this 15-minute break you will have to survive and prosper purely on your ability to fit in with the social patterns that operate in the playground. This is a tough world full of unspoken rules and regulations. For example, shadow network leaders who wield power using myriad behaviours and techniques; the subtle negotiation skills that require you to trade both toys and favours; your ability to fend off bullies; make sure that you are not the last person to be picked for a game of football; or the social pressure to conform with the 'right' branded clothes. It is the sophisticated capability to enter this world and forge social links which good networkers need to harness if they want to grow their social capital and make connections count.

I would really urge you to think back to that first day at school and the feeling that emerged as you entered the playground for the first time. It would be nice to think that this fear goes as we get older, but in my experience it doesn't. I still get this trepidation when I attend a conference, start a new job or walk into a room full of strangers. The difference now is that I know the apprehension will be there and simply develop strategies to manage the emotions. It is these strategies that form the backbone of the networking framework introduced in the book.

Social capitalization

We might describe social capital as the thoughts, feelings and behaviours contained within a group of people that can be called upon to create value. It can be seen in everyday situations in the allegiance and spirit that help a team of firefighters tackle a dangerous blaze; the thoughts, feelings and skills that enable your football team to win another cup (or not); or the shared experiences and beliefs that enable your local café to function effectively, even when the next stream of lorry drivers call in for the bacon sandwiches.

> We might describe social capital as the thoughts, feelings and behaviours contained within a group of people that can be called upon to create value.

You have it already in your various relationships with people who sit in your current network. When problems occur with your plumbing or electricity and there are no professionals around to help, then who would you call on? You might have four or five people who could and would help get you out of a problem. At work, are there people you operate with who, when push comes to shove, will help you to get the orders out in time? That is social capital, something that acts as glue for the personal capital that each person brings to the party and allows it to flow freely among the group so as to create value.

One of the things that people always mention when I raise the idea of networking is the fear that is it driven by self-interest rather than altruistic reasons. On the one hand, Francis Fukuyama suggests that social capital arises spontaneously as a product of iterated Prisoner's Dilemma games. Where a simple strategy of tit-for-tat (playing cooperation for cooperation and defection for defection) leads both players to a cooperative outcome. If individuals interact with each other repeatedly over time, they develop a stake in a reputation for honesty and reliability. He suggests that relationships based upon a society composed entirely of selfish people will develop social capital over time, simply because it makes sense to work to cooperate rather than in opposition.

However, I am not sure if I totally agree with this idea. I think the importance of the proposition is that it can legitimize the notion that successful networking can be based on selfish action. Yes, you are reading this book because you want to get, or improve your position in life or get promotion at work. Although there might be a few of you who are reading it to understand how to solve problems for other people (even then there might be a personal payback!), I guess this will be a small group. So

Networking is about doing better for yourself, but I hope that in the process you see the sense in my argument that you can only do better for yourself in the 'long run' with an intent to do better for other people as well.

networking is about doing better for yourself, but I hope that in the process you see the sense in my argument that you can only do better for yourself in the 'long run' with an intent to do better for other people as well. This is based on the simple principle that the generation of any social capital is built on the donation by two or more people in the relationships. They are donating their personal capital with anticipation that it will generate a return at some point downstream. Any investment process, no matter what form, can survive only if it is built on the premise that it is fair and equitable. If there is any notion that players in a trading relationship are out purely for self-interest, then greed, corruption and deceit will eventually creep in and in the long run destroy the trading system.

Social capital investment process

Now the suggestion that we might need to consider an 'investment process' when talking about the development of personal relationships might cause some people to throw their hands up in horror at the apparent coldness. However, please note two things: first, that this book is about professional networking, not social networking (there is no suggestion that you would follow any of these ideas in your personal life); second, most of the ideas in this section are things that many people do already, but at a tacit level and as such they are talked about only in private conversations or in hushed corners in the office. All this book seeks to do is to bring to the surface many of the undiscussible things that people talk about in private.

Investment criteria

As part of this investment process it makes sense to understand what criteria you will use to select potential partners in your network. This notion of investment criteria is a common activity in the financial markets as it seeks to achieve a fair and equitable return on its investment. The effective and astute investor will be able to:

- manage the investment process to optimize his/her return;
- reject any investment that will not give a good market return;
- identify investments that will take time to grow;

- find opportunities to derive synergies from future mergers and acquisition;
- spot potential to create synergies in the portfolio mix;
- provide limited seed capital for start up investment where there might be a marginal chance of return in the future;
- identify 'rising star' candidates in emerging markets;
- look for companies that demonstrate entrepreneurial vision;
- look for proven skills in their respective functional areas and relevant market or industry experience.

When applied to the idea of social capital investment, the same criteria might be considered. If you are going to use your valuable time to invest in a professional relationship, you might choose to use these criteria as a checklist, albeit implicitly. If we take the same financial criteria, we arrive at the following:

1. Ensure that you get the best from the social relationship.
2. Ensure that you don't create connections with negative people.
3. Don't rush a relationship – give it time to grow.
4. Find opportunities to derive synergies across your different networks.
5. Spot potential to create synergies between people within the current community.
6. Always be prepared to spend a little time with people even if you don't see a potential for connection at the moment.
7. Look out for good people and link up with them early on in their careers.
8. Try to connect with people who know where they are going and have a clear sense of purpose.
9. Try to connect with people who are skilled at what they do.

If your goal is to grow social capital that has sustainable value and will help achieve sustainable success, then you cannot keep drinking coffee with people for fun. Serious people are serious about how they network and the desire to reap a reward for the investment of their time in other people. This is where a set of personal criteria can help to ensure that you stay focused on the goal of social capital growth and not get distracted by the fact that you like the person. It is fine to like someone and want to spend time with that person, but it is also important to understand whether he or she is part of your professional network or personal social group.

> Serious people are serious about how they network and the desire to reap a reward for the investment of their time in other people.

Investment process

Once the investment choice has been made, there are various steps that can be followed to deliver a return on the financial investment. These steps are not mandatory or explicitly followed in every process, but the generic framework is common enough to indicate the type of processes that most investment journeys will follow as seen in Figure 2.1.

- **Asset**. This is the resource that the player has within the investment process. It might be land, money, access to other people, time or a whole array of different resources under our control.

- **Bank**. At some point before the investment begins we have to convert the asset or resources into working capital. The idea is to separate the tradable from the non-tradable items and bank it as an asset to be used for investment purposes.

- **Capital**. At this point the asset is now separated and is ready for investment. As working capital it will be affected by a number of forces. It will have a value applied to it (hard or arbitrary); it will be beset by risk (it can be enhanced or lost to the owner); and has notional ownership and as such can be transferred between owners.

- **Deal**. Once we have capital in place, we can make the capital work and so generate a profit. This is the trading stage where action is taken to make the capital dance. For the second-hand car trader, it is finding a punter off the street; for the stock broker, it is identifying the stock.

- **Earnings**. Once the deal or transaction is complete (in a perfect world), the original capital is recouped along with profit that compensates the owner for use of the capital. This is in the form of earnings. This might be a profit on the car sales, or an increase in stock value (or dividend)

Figure 2.1 Capital investment loop

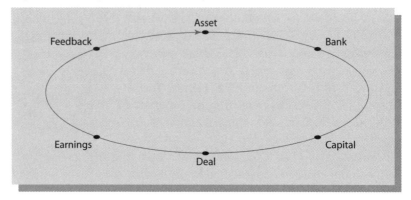

■ **Feedback**. In the final stage of the investment cycle, the owner can reinvest the earnings. The investor can either feed the earnings back into the investment loop or simply pull the combined capital and earnings out of the investment cycle and convert the new capital back into personal assets or resources.

The same process can be applied as you begin to invest in partners to join your network. You have assets in terms of access to people, you can capitalize these names, draw upon the capital and then receive a payback which in turn feeds value back into your personal asset base. This loop can be tracked against the social capital process as seen in Table 2.1.

The important things to consider with respect to the social investment strategies are:

■ You will often need some seed corn capital to start with. This might be your existing contact list, a list of names from the last conference you attended or the people you worked with in the last three jobs.

■ You will need to consider the list and separate out those people who are part of the tradable process and those that you do not wish to include as professional social capital (maybe friends and family). The bank stage is critical here because you have to ask serious questions

Table 2.1 The social capital process

	Financial investment *Car purchase and resale*	Social network *Career change*
Asset	House as asset	List of names in personal diary
Bank	Short-term mortgage taken on house to use as foundation for business	Select top 10 names from list and put into a file index
Capital	Money raised in mortgage becomes capital to buy rare E-Type Jag	Names in file list become capital investment to develop career change network
Deal	Jag sold to rich overseas millionaire	Contact each person and explain that you require career change and would like to enlist his or her help
Earn	100% profit on sale	Payback in form of recommendation from two people, which leads to interview
Feedback	Mortgage paid off and profit used to build extension on house	New job attained and new role used to increase social contacts

about the extent to which you are willing to trade on personal friendships. I believe that it is often this stage that creates the most emotional tension for people. When they can't separate the two types of relationship the result is that they decide that networking is not for them or make silly mistakes and end up abusing the social relationship with their friends and family.

■ You need to have the stomach to trade in the social market. It can be quite an intellectual and emotional challenge if you are not used to seeing relationships as bankable assets. If you are unable to accept this idea, then your professional network may well end up as a social network rather than social capital.

■ You must be prepared to reinvest any gain back into the network. If you keep draining the pond, one day it will be empty. In the same way, you cannot keep taking from your social capital pool. You must be prepared to reinvest by giving time and energy back to fuel the flow of contacts and goodwill.

■ There is risk as well as reward in this investment process. You might spend a great deal of time investing in one relationship only to see it collapse as the individual retires to another country. You should be as careful with social investment decisions as you would when taking out a pension or mortgage.

If this appears overly clinical, it is only because we are not used to deconstructing how we interact with people and, in particular, how we interact to achieve selfish personal goals. People often react against the idea of networking because they associate it with the dodgy connotations of 'knowing the right people', a distaste for 'Machiavellian politics', because they don't want to kiss up to the powerful or because networking stops you from 'doing work that really adds value'. People may accuse you of all sorts of awful things because you admit to having a strategy for networking. However, no matter what you call it, we all do it! Often people see others who network well and assume that they have a magic wand that helps them to grow contacts everywhere they go. In most cases they don't, they just know how to make their personal connections count. The hard reality is that who you know often does count for more than what you know.

> If you keep draining the pond, one day it will be empty. You must be prepared to reinvest by giving time and energy back to fuel the flow of contacts and goodwill.

Is the prime minister or president of the United States the most knowledgeable about domestic problems, world order, social problems or economic theory? No, (hardly) they get other people to do that, as their primary skill is the capacity to build alliances in a political network that is naturally suspicious and potentially corrupt. It is this capability to make connections count that helps them get to the top of their profession and remain effective once in post. Interestingly it is often the failure to maintain this capability that can lead to their demise. As we see so often, it only needs a small amount of mismanagement for the social pack to turn against the leader and then they come crashing down.

The fact is that in any society, be it business, politics, school or even the neighbourhood watch, connections count. If the fact that I can get a few people together and form a neighbourhood watch to keep an eye on each other's homes is manipulative or wrong then, sorry, but if it lowers the crime rate in my neighbourhood, keeps my house safe and increases the market value of my property, then I will carry on doing it. In the same way, if I can work with people who can help take my personal capital to market and I can reciprocate and help find exposure for theirs, that sounds like a shared success to me. So long as we are open and ethical in the process and do not veer into a secret society, then what is good for us must be better for the community (social or business).

Social cost

A friend of mine was an avid networker. He was the consummate social animal and excelled at it. He would use his professional links to build up a great network of contacts and as such had an amazing stock of social capital that he could call upon until he landed a great job with a major league big blue-chip company. This was *the* job he had been working for and there he was doing what he wanted, travelling the world and being seen as an expert in his field. A year passed and we couldn't really get to see each other because he was busy.

The problem was that while his stock of air miles was increasing, his stock of social capital was diminishing at an alarming rate. All of a sudden he realized that his network had been eroded. He didn't have time to keep in touch with anyone, didn't attend conferences, didn't act as a conduit to broker relationships between people and didn't really know what was going on outside his specialist field of interest. He had failed to maintain the continual investment in his social capital because the cost seemed too high at the time.

My challenge to him was, what would happen if the company were to make you redundant? How would you get a new job? Who could you call upon to help meet the right people, and to what extent can you demonstrate that you are in tune with the wider market rather than just your niche area? The answer was that he couldn't. He had, in effect, suddenly moved from being in control of his destiny by virtue of the network that he operated and instead had become a corporate slave, locked into the social capital of the company he kept and which kept him.

The problem is that you cannot just go out and buy more social capital. The investment process takes a long time, and the gap between re-accumulation of the social capital and the current situation can leave you very exposed to the political and commercial whims of your masters and markets. It is very easy to decide not to paint the house windows this year because the cost of paint and time is too high. However, the downstream cost as the wood begins to rot will be much higher in the long run. Any decision not to invest in your professional network now is potentially driving up your downstream cost.

Social corruption

As a final thought, it is important not to get carried away with the notion that social capital is always good. What is effective and positive social capital in one situation or market can be quite the opposite in another.

Consider the neighbourhood watch that supports the local community in one context and how it can become a vehicle for vigilante action when a suspected offender moves into the neighbourhood. Work associations that enable efficient wage bargaining and safety practices in one month can soon turn into confrontational groups which seek to attack the management body or, as we can see peace protesters, seeking to bring about the elimination of world debt can turn into groups that take violent action and cause pain and injury to groups that oppose their viewpoint. The important point here is that for any of these groups that have apparently developed a negative bias in their social agenda, it is often not the whole group that causes the problem. With the best overall intentions, agendas can be hijacked, so it is not the whole of trade unions which attack management (or vice versa). Social networks are powerful systems that have great value but are rarely regulated. As such, it takes only a few people to impact how the social group looks to the outside world.

> What is effective and positive social capital in one situation or market can be quite the opposite in another.

Thus, social capital also has an important 'down side'. Where you have communities, teams or associations which work at cross-purposes to society's best interest, they can actually hinder economic and social development. The original idea to do well through social grouping can instead become corrupted, as the group turns insular and views the outside group as the opposition or in some cases the enemy. The net result is one of alienation and exclusion for the broader social group they set out to support.

Always try to step inside out and ensure that your social capital is being used for positive social or commercial purposes and that it has not been hijacked to suit the ends of subtle fifth columnists. Think about the networks at work. When in an informal setting do you run the company down and collectively point out the faults of the bosses (whilst not telling them to their faces) or do you use the generative power of the group to reflect on ways to help the business? If so, you might have drifted into a model in which you are socially excluding people without realizing it. This is a dangerous point and one that you are well advised to avoid as you grow your network.

The danger is when the level of exclusion spreads across the entire community like a virus and becomes accepted as the norm. It is this social virus that leads to the collapse of companies when they forge unethical relationships with the external auditors, the destruction of sports teams when they become corrupt and take backhanders from bookies, or corruption in the education field when teachers deliberately cheat to get children through the exams. In many cases the virus starts by infecting a few people who adopt opposing social beliefs that have a destructive impact on the external world. The risk is where this virus becomes really contagious and spreads throughout the community without any chance to restrict the flow.

> Never forget that the accumulation of social capital gives you social rights and this automatically confers social responsibility.

In all these cases the social group has taken itself too seriously and excluded the civic and ethical responsibilities that it owes to the wider social group. This is a real danger that arises with any social network and it is one that you must be very careful of as your network begins to grow and create social capital of some value. Never forget that the accumulation of social capital gives you social rights and this automatically confers social responsibility. You must share joint accountability with fellow network members to ensure that this responsibility is discharged with fairness and integrity. Failure to do this will seed the process of well-deserved self-destruction.

'One of the principles of networking is to become visible whilst generating intellectual capital, then attracting networkers to you (the honey and the bee principle). There are ways of using conferences to do this. I began by deciding to be headhunted three years ago, fought my way onto conference agendas by ringing up and asking why I hadn't been invited to speak (didn't they know who I was?); asked who had dropped out as speaker, and offered to do a presentation to their prescription. One busy weekend later, I had a presentation, and never looked back.'

Victor Newman

Network frame

It can be quite a challenge to fully master all the necessary actions and behaviours that are required to successfully build a professional network. However, it is possible to take many of the key elements and break them down into a series of components that make connections count.

The networking model used in this book is built around two core elements. The first is that all effective networking is based on three human dimensions: *behavioural*, having to do with activity and doing; the *affective*, having to do with feelings, emotions, values and motivation; and the *cognitive*, having to do with thinking and believing. This model is not new or unique. It is the basic psychological view of man that goes back to the Greeks and probably the Egyptians. It views man as composed of three interdependent processes. All are interdependent, and no one part can change without the other parts also changing.

> All effective networking is based on three human dimensions: behavioural, affective and cognitive.

The second element considers what factors are seen to be important by both practitioners and academics in the formation of social capital and the management of professional networks. They are:

- Sustainable relationships are founded on a win/win mentality.
- The ability to build an effective social relationship is at the heart of any networking process.
- As the size of a network increases in size and complexity, it will need careful management to maintain its currency and coherence.
- Any professional community is a marketplace where people need to promote themselves and their services.
- Trust is the oil that lubricates the network; without this, knowledge and goodwill will cease to flow.

■ All social systems are subject to the second law of thermodynamics which argues that there can never be a perpetual motion machine, so all networks will try to decay once constructed.

It is important to stress that management of these six factors does not guarantee the formation of an effective professional network, but there is a good chance that a failure to address these issues will lead to a network that is difficult to manage and does not help realize the value it might for all members.

Networking elements

We all use three different aspects of ourselves when we network – the affective or heart elements, cognitive or head aspects, and behavioural or hand elements. Three-dimensional networking means that you draw upon the 'whole you' to create relationships. In essence, you bring together the three key elements of how you feel, think and behave (or heart, head and hand) to forge highly effective social relationships.

(a) **Heart dimension.** This is the emotional epicentre that provides the inner strength and compass of the natural networker. It drives the belief in true networking where the goal is to deliver a win for both parties and also help to drive the inner motivation to get close to people at an emotional level as opposed to a superficial one. The two key attributes in the heart dimension of the model are:

– **Activate abundance.** Recognize that you have value to offer other people and they have value in return, irrespective of job

Figure 3.1   The three networking dimensions

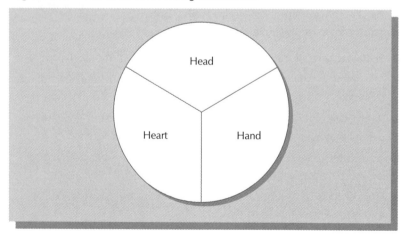

title, flash car or position. If you start to recognize the abundant value that can be created in any relationship and then help the other person to recognize this, there is a greater chance that he or she will welcome your offer to socialize.

- **Build a bridge**. At the end of the day the development of a professional network means that at some point in time you might have to walk across the crowded conference floor and start a conversation with complete strangers. To move from a cold relationship and creating some degree of rapport in a limited amount of time. Like it or not, it is a fundamental skill for anyone who wishes to grow his/her professional network. All relationships will start at the indifferent level, simply because you don't know each other. Your job is to use all your social skills to move from a distant or inactive relationship to one that is social and highly interactive.

(b) **Head dimension**. The head function remains above our emotional needs and helps formulate plans and make decisions relating to how we network. Effective head orientation will produce natural networkers who take a broad, aerial view of life and who have, as a result, a rich and varied perspective on things. They will also be adaptable and able to change how they network according to the environment they find themselves in. The two key attributes in the head dimension of the model are:

> You will need to ensure that you know who is in your network, who isn't in your network, who shouldn't be in your network and who you want in it. To do this you will need the skills of a cartographer, to implicitly or explicitly chart your network as it was, is and will be.

- **Chart the connections**. As your network grows you will need to ensure that you know who is in your network, who isn't in your network, who shouldn't be in your network and who you want in it. To do this you will need the skills of a cartographer, to implicitly or explicitly chart your network as it was, is and will be.

- **Dare to be different**. There is little point in building a large network of people if they don't remember who you are or what you do and hence never call you. A critical goal within any networking process is to create personal stickiness. Understand how to keep to the front of your colleagues' minds. One way to do this is to help them understand how you are different from everyone else in their network and, in particular, what level of rich variety you can add to their personal capital.

A critical goal within any networking process is to create personal stickiness. Understand how to keep to the front of your colleagues' minds.

(c) **Hand dimension**. Natural networkers exhibit two core behaviours. They are able to let go of their precious ego and feel safe enough for their network colleagues to play with their brand in the market. They also have the ability and desire to maintain and refuel the network once it has been established. The two key attributes in the hand dimension of the model are:

− *Entrust each other*. By creating a network link with someone, you are entrusting to that person your brand and personal reputation. This is not something to be given or taken lightly. You need to be conscious of the extent to which you are lending your brand to others and when others are lending their brand to you. Failure to understand the fragility of the trust in a network can cause it to collapse overnight.

− *Fuel the flow*. As with any system, maintenance normally has to start on the day after it is built. This is not because your network has a fault, simply because it is an organic system and all systems in this universe have a natural tendency to entropy or decay. So you need to set aside time to care and maintain your network on a regular basis.

Figure 3.2 Network frame

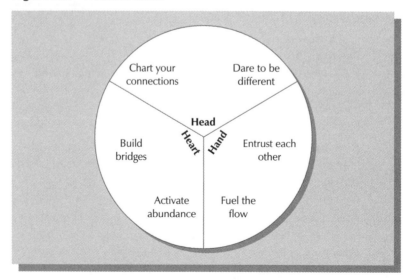

This framework is not offered as a definite *'this is how you must network'* model. It is simply a pulling together of a number of things that effective networkers do automatically, and which aspiring networkers might want to think about.

'As our culture changes from a society of "joiners" (Grange, Rotary Club, Masons, Kiwanis, Lions Club, etc.) to a society of networkers, this "Abundance" is the thread that must link parties together, rather than a fancy fez, incantation, and secret handshake.'

G. Matthew Bulley

'The investment in time and energy creating a network will only be worthwhile if you are genuinely interested in the people in it – sustaining it for purely selfish reasons won't work.'

Angela Abell

Activate abundance

Social abundance is the belief that $2 + 2 = 5$, that there is enough cake for everyone, and that you can give and the get will come later. It is the thought that 'of course it makes sense to give because the selfish society will ultimately kill itself'. It is the great feeling that comes when you have helped someone out or someone has taken time out to help you; and it is how you behave when your best friend has just been dumped and you give her your last chocolate bar.

> So often I see networking viewed as a process to manage the Rolodex and grow the revenue stream quickly. Yes you can do that – but just watch as you rapidly reduce the value of your social capital once your peers get wise and discard you and your relationship.

The whole ethos of natural networking must be grounded in an abundance mentality. This is unlike some networking approaches, which hint very strongly at the 'screw others to get rich quick' approach. So often I see networking viewed as a process to manage the Rolodex and grow the revenue stream quickly. Yes you can do that – but just watch as you rapidly reduce the value of your social capital once your peers get wise and discard you and your relationship.

Think of the relationships where you feel that the other person uses you or vice versa. You may have a network connection, but what sustainable value does it offer? When really in a mess you might call that person for help, or he/she might drop you a line asking for help, but this is often at desperation point and the clock will be ticking. The call for help will have been logged and the debt will be called in, probably when you are least able to free up time.

This chapter addresses the questions that we all have to consider as we start to build our capacity to generate social abundance:

(a) Do I understand the value I have and can offer to the network?

(b) How can we use the abundance idea to treat all people with an abundant mindset and not just those from whom we need something in return?

(c) How can we measure and understand the level of abundance in any of our relationships?

(d) How do we create abundance with people we don't want to be associated with?

(e) How do we create abundance by tapping into areas beyond our immediate network?

Self abundance

■ We are all born with at least one unique gift – the first trick is to believe it, the second to find it and the third to use it.

■ Let yourself wallow in your own abundance.

At its very heart, networking is founded on the desire to share your value with other people: to be bountiful and offer others an insight into how you think, feel and behave. However, it can be pretty difficult to offer something if you don't think you have anything to give. I consistently meet people who either can't or won't network and the primary cause is self-doubt about their personal value.

> It can be pretty difficult to offer something if you don't think you have anything to give. I consistently meet people who either can't or won't network and the primary cause is self-doubt about their personal value.

I had an awful experience like this once where I froze at a key moment. In the early stages of building my business I was fortunate enough to be invited to present a workshop at a large and prodigious conference in Rome. This is the situation that any aspiring author dreams of. The chance to work with people of a like mind who have taken the trouble to meet and share stories about themselves, their beliefs and what they do. If ever there was a networking heaven then this was it. Even the blurb about the event promoted the fact that long lunches and coffee breaks were set up just to let people meet and greet.

So there I was in the middle of a room full of people who 'potentially' wanted to meet me and I froze. The inner alarm bells rang, I got scared and just couldn't talk to anyone. My only way out was to find one or two people I vaguely knew and latch on to them like a limpet. In this way I was able to 'look engaged' as if I was 'networking'. Even after surviving this ordeal it went from bad to worse.

There was one guy, a famous expert in my field who was at the event. I was desperate to meet him to talk about areas that we might have in common. Even better when I sat at the dinner table, there he was sitting next but one to me. Could I pluck up the courage to say hello – like hell I could. I spent all my time talking to everyone but him. Even crazier is the fact that I went back to the hotel room that night and sent him an e-mail saying what a shame it was that we didn't get a chance to meet. Sad or what?

Although there were many reasons for my abysmal failure to meet this guy, the core problem was that I didn't believe in my own self-abundance. I just didn't think and feel that he would want to meet me. Now I know that it was crazy but at the time a limited view of my self-abundance took over and the inner rudder took me towards the rocks of oblivion.

If this is such a simple process, why does it go wrong? Why do people find it so difficult to build this emotional bridge? Why does networking fail to deliver real bridging opportunities? Often it is less about a failure in the ideas that people are trying to share or their networking skills; it is because we all suffer from some level of personal insecurity. So many of us have a niggling lack of confidence about ourselves. As a result, we hold back from really exposing ourselves to other people.

Do you ever feel you're not good enough to just walk up and talk to a stranger about yourself? That feeling of 'why would they be interested in me?' If so, this insecurity is a figment of your imagination, manufactured by you. Its driver is routed in the curse of self-doubt, the sense that you're not good enough to do things that others believe you capable of. Everywhere I meet people this curse of insecurity seems to permeate and is an emotional cancer that wreaks havoc for people who really want to be successful in their personal and professional life.

> This networking frame is based on the idea that you can discard any notion of dependence on titles and badges of office, that you can shift from insecurity to *in*-security and decide that you have value and that other people will get value by association with you.

So often when I try to help people develop their natural networking capability they will say: 'but he is the chief executive of a large corporation and I am just a technician – he won't want to talk to me'. In this case the badge of office is conferring the legitimacy and power to talk to someone. They are only looking at the title and forgetting that underneath is a person just the same as them, someone who often suffers the same insecurities and self doubt (and in many cases more).

This networking frame is based on the idea that you can discard any notion of dependence on titles and badges of office, that you can shift from insecurity to *in*-security and decide that you have value and that other people will get value by association with you.

You may be one of the lucky ones who don't suffer from this self doubt. If, however, you do suffer from any of the thoughts or feelings that I have described, then I urge you to take time out to understand this demon, where it has come from and what you are going to do about it. You might not be able to kill it, but you can tame and manage it. But this takes time and energy and can be quite daunting in the process. However, once the demon is challenged and tamed, a whole new life can open up in front of you, one where you are not scared to be you and help others understand the value you can offer.

Sow before you reap

- It is often cheaper to buy something when you don't need it rather than when you are desperate.
- 'Plant a kernel of wheat and you reap a pint; plant a pint and you reap a bushel. Always the law works to give you back more than you give.'

Anthony Norvell

There is a wonderful film called 'Pay it Forward' about a boy who is given a school assignment to think of something he could do to change the world. He suggests that we each do a good turn for three people. They in turn have to 'pay it forward', i.e. do the same for other people. The essence is to simply do a favour for another person – without any expectation of being paid back. The unconditional favour can be large or small. It doesn't have to be a big thing. It can just seem that way, depending on whom you do it for.

Think about your personal and professional life. Take stock of all the assets, ideas, stock, contacts, equipment or any other resource that sits under your control. Now think of three people in your life who could do with a hand. *Note* – not a hand out. This is a hand up, one person taking the time and energy to spread some good to someone else. Now if you think of these three people, is there anything within your domain that might be of value to them but has little real value to you? Can you lend them some equipment while they try to build a business? Can you put them in touch with a relative of yours who has some important contacts in the area that they want to work in? Or when walking down the street, do you have a spare coin for a homeless person? All of these things might mean virtually nothing to you but can make a world of difference to the other person.

If you are able to give without any immediate expectation of a return on your investment then payback will often come in other ways. The more you take an abundant view of the world, the more people will start to recognize that you are not just out for self-interest, that you are happy to invest in their life without calling two weeks later for a return favour, and it signals your ethics without you having to say anything. Once people understand that you have an abundant attitude, they will stop competing with you and instead seek to collaborate on projects; they will be prepared to give support to you without any obligation or pressure to return the favour; and doors will open in new places because people understand that self-interest is not your primary interest.

Finally, abundance is not something you can just 'think' about doing. There must be congruence between your head and heart in the way you seek to give before getting. You probably know people who speak the carefully crafted words of abundance, but when push comes to shove, self-interest is seen as their driving goal. Where this happens the notional idea of sustainable networking will collapse in a pile of acrimony, back-biting and ruined reputations.

Level of abundance

- One small abundant act for you may be a life-changing act for someone else.
- 'The test of our progress is not whether we add to the abundance of those who have much. It is whether we provide enough to those who have little.   *'Franklin Delano Roosevelt*

Professional networking that is selfish and short-lived is not sustainable networking. The only real form of networking is one founded on the notion of shared and sustainable outcomes. The key to this choice is the absolute focus on mutual benefit and the generation of shared success through networking.

However, you can only really achieve shared success if you understand what success means for yourself and others. I often see people who try to achieve a shared outcome but the trouble is that they don't take the time to really understand what the other person wants to achieve. They are focused on achieving their goal and pay little attention to the other person's needs and desires. The end result teeters between a battle of wills as each person struggles to assert his/her view of success, or lacklustre output because no one has really said what is important for them. Only by understanding what real success is for the people we work and live with can we hope to achieve sustainable success with them.

The way to do this is to keep two ideas in mind. First is the need for constant enquiry – to understand other people's goals, dreams and desires, by showing consideration and trying to understand what success means for them. Second, the need for advocacy – to make sure that other people know what you want and need by having the courage to tell them. Once you understand these two dimensions you can appreciate how your needs and their needs interrelate and where you can start to find synergies in the abundance. The balance and relationship between these two processes can be seen in Figure 4.1.

> Only by understanding what real success is for the people we work and live with can we hope to achieve sustainable success with them.

Figure 4.1   Shared success model

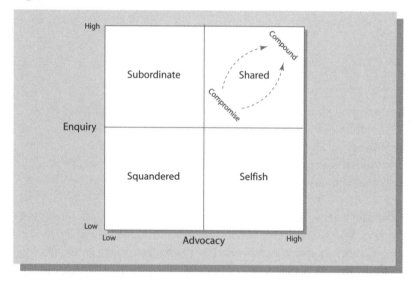

- **Squandered**. In this relationship little is happening. You might have links in place and invest time in each other, but the end result is that neither person is incurring any capital growth. You might send each other the occasional e-mail to say hello, but there is little activity on either side to grow the personal or social capital.

    For example, imagine two team managers. One runs the sales team and the other the service team. They are both fiercely competitive and want promotion. However, they both take a scarcity mentality at work and spend most of their time trying to ensure that the other person is not seen as more successful than them. The net result is a wasted opportunity, where what could be a productive relationship for them both has been squandered because neither takes the time to listen to what the other person wants to achieve.

- **Subordinate**. In this relationship value is being created, but you are not getting any of it. The emphasis is on giving benefit without any focus on what you will gain from the relationship.

  Building on the previous story, the sales manager realizes that he needs to resolve the problem because senior managers are starting to comment on the problems surfacing between the two teams. So he talks to the service manager and tries to understand what they need and how he can help resolve their problems. This is great for the service manager, but it still doesn't lead to shared success or a higher level of abundance.

- **Selfish**. This is the inverse of the subordinate level, where you do the taking, without giving anything back. Your personal capital is being multiplied by use of the network link, but it isn't renewable and sustainable because other people will eventually have enough of your demands and exploitation. (Unless they too are doormat wannabes.)

  After a while the sales manager gets fed up with the situation and focuses instead on telling the service manager what he wants from her, how she can change the team's process to help optimize the sales team's performance. In this case one team might improve but the level of shared abundance does little to improve.

- **Shared**. At this level, you are both gaining value from the relationship, but it is additive in nature. So there is give and get in this relationship but little growth or synergy because ideas and favours are being traded rather than developed.

  Finally, the sales and service managers decide to sit down and work together. They both spend time listening to the other person's issues and explaining their position. They reach a compromise position where they start to reduce some of the problems between the teams and ensure that the members of the senior team don't see them in a bad light.

- **Synergistic**. This is shared success at a compound level. This type of relationship is where two people spend time together and in doing so create something that exceeds the sum of their two parts. The formal definition might be: 'The interaction of two or more agents or forces so that their combined effect is greater than the sum of their individual effects'.

So finally the sales and service managers take time to really understand what the other person wants on a personal and business level and share their deep concerns and goals. By understanding each other's work they start to synergize and find ways for the teams to work at optimum efficiency. By creating this compound relationship the chances increase that both will achieve their goals rather than just one person beating the other in a promotion race.

> If you choose to spend time with someone on a project, you're using valuable time, energy and ideas. You can't afford to give such resources away if the relationship is going to operate at a level of compromise.

Within the shared area it is important to understand what synergistic options exist with the other person. The most effective network relationship is where a number of people want to share ideas, collaborate to develop them and collectively create an answer. The net result is a compound or synergistic relationship, when the sum of the parts is greater than the whole. This is such a simple idea but often overlooked. Most people wouldn't even consider investing their financial savings into an account where the end of year return delivered the same amount. We expect the bank to invest our money wisely into the market and to return interest on a compound basis. In the same way, if we plan to invest our time and energy in the creation of social capital, then we need to ensure that it is multiplied through association with others, and not eroded in value as it circulates around the network.

This synergistic or compound relationship is an important factor in the networking model. So often people invest in relationships that produce nothing more than the sum of the parts. If you choose to spend time with someone on a project, you're using valuable time, energy and ideas. You can't afford to give such resources away if the relationship is going to operate at a level of compromise. Instead, you want to work with people who take your ideas and build on them and whose ideas you can build on. The net result is a compound relationship, where the sum of the parts is greater than the whole.

Compound relationships

Compound networking is founded on two principles: 'exposed advocacy' (where you're prepared to expose your criteria with other people) and 'empathic enquiry' (where your goal is to use a questioning structure that enables the other person to expose his/her inner personal success criteria).

Where both principles are employed a shift is made from compromise to compound success.

Exposed advocacy:

- **Expose private wins**. Have a clear and focused understanding of what good means to you. How would you define success from your perspective and how can you make it clear enough for others to understand?

- **Discuss undiscussibles**. The essence of exposed advocacy is to move to the surface the shadow desires, to feel comfortable enough to expose and explain to another person the deep personal factors that really drive your behaviour.

- **Welcome debate**. Offer others the chance to explore and understand the ideas being put forward. Unless the other person feels able to explore the success factors you're aiming for, there is a chance that he/she won't fully understand what the aims are and how they can be achieved.

Empathic enquiry:

- **Choose to listen**. This might sound silly, but it's the conscious desire to put the tacit receptors into gear and to listen with your heart. This is a very specific and conscious process, not something that might automatically happen as you're walking along the corridor chatting to someone. As any parent knows, it is easy to answer superficially yes and no when a child is constantly asking questions. This can happen at work where we switch to autopilot and just talk to people at a surface level whilst processing our important issues internally. Sometimes we have to turn the inner voice off and listen with our whole self.

- **Minimize internal distractions**. As we listen to other people describe their goals it's easy for the inner voice to jump in and challenge or disagree with the statement being made. Your inner voice must be tightly managed to ensure it doesn't corrupt the inflow of thoughts and feelings from the other person. The next time you are listening to someone who is presenting you with a case or argument to do something that you don't agree with, listen to your inner voice. There is every chance that the moment you 'know' what the other person is about to say you will begin to formulate your answer, and then get into a holding pattern ready to launch your return salvo before he/she has a chance to pause for breath. The problem with this is that you have missed over 50% of what the person is saying, and this might be the most important element. The trick is to turn this inner voice off so that it no longer presents a distraction.

■ **Love paradox**. You must be able to agree with the speaker's wish to achieve a set of goals, even if you don't agree with the actual goals. This is the art of listening without prejudice and accepting other people's wishes without acting as critic.

■ **Manage air space**. You must stay conscious of the balance between listening and telling, as there is always competition for air space. Try to ensure that the balance is appropriate for the outcome you wish to achieve. Don't formulate an answer in your head before the person has finished speaking and wherever possible leave space in the conversation to allow the other person room to play with an idea that he or she has just exposed.

> The essence of exposed advocacy is to move to the surface the shadow desires, to feel comfortable enough to expose and explain to another person the deep personal factors that really drive your behaviour .

The shift from compromise to compound success is based on your ability and desire to take the advocacy and enquiry dimensions to the limit. If the network relationship isn't reaching its full potential, are you really using the full power of exposed advocacy and empathic enquiry? Is all your energy and passion focused on extracting from the other person their personal success criteria and helping that person understand your own?

The highest level of interaction is where the communication between groups of people produces compound outcomes, and the creation of social capital by the amplification of people's ideas. As people expose their thoughts, ideas and personal patterns, so the level of understanding and social capital within the room will expand.

Love the one you're with?

■ Effective networking doesn't mean that you have to compromise your personal values or ethics.

■ If you wouldn't have beer or coffee with someone, then maybe you shouldn't network with that person.

One major dilemma that occurs in any networking process is: 'I really need your help – but I don't like you'! What do you do when faced with a situation where you need to network with someone you don't like? The person might be a bigot, someone who left your sister up the aisle, or scrounged drinks off you for the last two years. Maybe just being in the same room as this individual brings you out in a cold sweat, or you just yearn to blurt out how you really feel. But what happens when you discover that he or she has access to someone else who can help you with a major problem at work or get the promotion you are desperate for?

> What do you do when faced with a situation where you need to network with someone whom you don't like? One of the ways to reduce this tension is to break the situation down into a series of options and choices.

This situation can lead to a great deal of tension. Tension for you as you worry about 'do I' or 'don't I' decisions; tension for the other person because he or she is not sure why you will not join the network; and tension between you because of the undiscussibles that don't get surfaced. One of the ways to reduce this tension is to break the situation down into a series of options and choices as seen in Figure 4.2.

The decision tree in Figure 4.2 tries to classify the choices that can be made when you are placed in such a difficult state of affairs. When faced with the situation where you have someone you are not happy to work with, you have one of four options:

Figure 4.2 Network partner choices

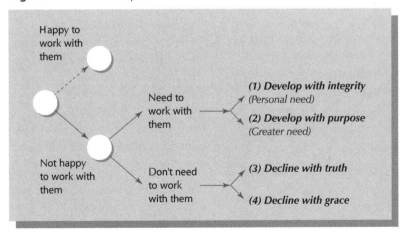

■ Need to work with them

(1) *Develop with integrity*. Often we might decide to work with someone we don't want to work with because it will help us to achieve certain personal goals. This is a common situation that we all face at different times. At a Christmas dinner, we meet our partner's boss who turns out to be loud and offensive, but it is important to support our partner and so make the best of a bad situation.

(2) *Develop with purpose*. Sometimes we really would sooner not work with someone but choose to put up with the situation because of a greater good. This might be a decision to undertake some charity work by working with a local prison to help coach the inmates who are about to be released. In doing this you might be faced with someone who you find morally offensive and who acts against everything you stand for. However, you decide to look at the greater good and work on the basis that your choice is designed to help the person change and only by working with him/her will you be able to help the person develop in the long run.

■ Don't need to work with them

(3) *Decline with truth*. In this case you decide that you are unable to network with the person and decide to tell him or her why. This is a difficult call to make because you have to know why you are making the undiscussible discussible. Are you revealing your dislike because you want to dump your feelings or do you believe that there is an ethical reason why it is important to say why you cannot work together.

(4) *Decline with grace*. With this choice you make the decision not to work with the person but to not tell the person the real reason for the lack of engagement. Again, only you can make the choice, but sometimes there is little benefit for either party in giving unsolicited feedback and it is easier to withdraw from the relationship with grace and discretion.

> If you don't think about where you would draw the line in the sand before you come cross a situation, how will you know when you have crossed it?

Life is about managing trade-offs and so is managing networks. In an ideal world you could form a really effective network that consists purely of people that you like and want to spend time with. However, life is rarely like that. Unless you have an independent source of income and don't really need the benefits of a professional network, there will be people who you need to associate with but are less keen on. The trick is to understand the trade-offs you are prepared to make before building the network so that you don't get yourself into potentially embarrassing and complex relationships. If you don't think about where you would draw the line in the sand before you come across a situation, how will you know when you have crossed it?

Slingshot – use your net's net

- The level of abundance doesn't just come from you and your net, it also comes from your net's net.
- The only limiting factor in how far you spread your net is your ability and energy to throw the mesh.

After spending time building and managing the network you should have a robust and solid platform in place. However, networking is all about leverage. Its core purpose is to optimize your personal capital in the market by sharing and socializing what you have with other people so that they can in turn share and socialize your capital with their network. If this is the case, then it will pay to understand what networks your members are part of and how you can leverage this cross connection. The goal is to bridge from where you are to where you want to be using the easiest path.

Imagine a spacecraft that has to travel to Jupiter but which can't take a direct path because it would require too much fuel. Instead, the craft follows complex roundabout routes called 'tours' that take it past various planets and moons. Those bodies provide 'gravity assists', commonly called 'slingshot' trajectories, which enable the spacecraft to achieve the proper speed and heading as seen in Figure 4.3.

As the spacecraft approaches a planet it is attracted by its gravity, speeds up (with respect to the planet), flies past (it's moving fast enough so it isn't held captive by the planet), slows down again as it's attracted by the planet's gravity and continues on its way. Net change in speed with respect to the planet: zero. But it has had its course changed by the slingshot effect caused by the planet's gravity. It is now flying in a different direction than it was before and with no additional fuel expenditure by the spacecraft.

It's a bit like grabbing hold of a handrail as you run down a flight of stairs to turn yourself quickly to reach the next flight of stairs heading down – you change direction by doing so. This was essential for the Ulysses spacecraft, which used a slingshot around the planet Jupiter to change its flight path out of the plane of the ecliptic (the plane in which the Earth and planets orbit around the Sun) into a polar orbit around the Sun. No spacecraft could carry enough propellants to do this with a rocket engine firing alone.

Figure 4.3 Slingshot trajectory

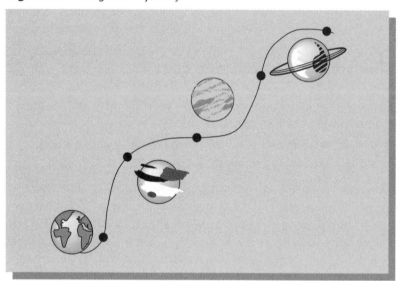

Figure 4.4 Network slingshots

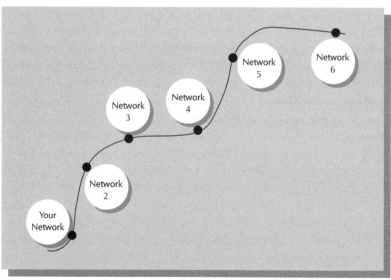

In the same way, a key part of the networking model is to use the associated networks to slingshot through various connections. The idea is to understand whom you would like to get in touch with as the final point of contact. Once you have a clear destination, it becomes a simple matter to plot a path to them using all your various connections as the slingshots.

Now although this might sound difficult, it is actually far easier than most people realize to get from point to point, even to people who seem very inaccessible or remote. The world is getting smaller all the time. With the explosion in network technology it is now possible to bridge a contact with almost anyone who has an e-mail address. The result is that the degree of separation between you and people you want to meet has been reduced. The small-world phenomenon formalizes the anecdotal notion that 'you are only ever six "degrees of separation" away from anybody else on the planet'. Thus, even when two people do not have a friend in common, only a short chain of links separates them.

This is neatly encapsulated in the Kevin Bacon Game. A computer scientist suggested that Kevin (not a major league star) was at the centre of the movie industry.[3] He did this by challenging people to think about the following:

- Think of an actor or actress.
- If he/she has ever been in a film with Kevin Bacon, he/she has a 'Bacon Number' of one.
- If the actor/actress has never been in a film with Kevin Bacon but has been in a film with somebody else who has, that represents a Bacon Number of two, and so on.

He suggested that no one who has been in an American film ever has a Bacon Number of greater than four. Elvis Presley, for example, has a Bacon Number of two. This may seem nothing more than a weird fact about a weird industry, but the suggestion is that it is a very strong example of an observable fact.

Try not to think of your initial network as 'the network'. Your potential network is the world and the current domain is just the launch vehicle that can give you access to your worldwide professional network. This really is abundance mentality taken to its fullest possible extent. This is where you see the world as your oyster and once you have that mindset then it really can become a global professional network.

As an example, think of your organization or workplace. Now imagine the one person who is farthest from your reach but with whom you would love to make contact. Using a diagram like the one shown in Figure 4.5, place yourself on the left-hand side and the person you would like to bridge with on the right-hand side. Start to think about who you know that will move you closer to that person. Alternatively, think of the people who know the target and start to consider if any of them are close to you. One important thing is that the most obvious route may not be the optimum one. It might be that someone in your network who works in a totally different company may know someone who knows that person. So try to be really divergent in your thinking and spread out all the possible combinations that will get to the target.

In the same way that extending your network can massively explode the value of your personal capital, expanding beyond your bounded network can take the level of amplification even further. However, netting-your-net takes energy and courage. Don't enter it lightly and with the expectation that you can generate quick wins. However, when it works, the payback on the investment can be quite phenomenal.

Figure 4.5 Slingshot map

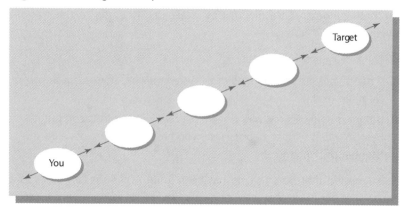

In summary

Ask yourself:

- Do I really value myself and present this to the world with confidence?
- Do I take time to understand how other people see the world and modify my behaviour to put them at ease?
- Do I seek to achieve real compound value from all my relationships?
- Do I know what my line in the sand is – who I will work with, who I won't and why?
- Do I know how to use my connections networks to create value?

'The way I used to teach it to highfliers was to get them to map the internal and external influence markets, and then what it took to get in, who was already in there who could get you in, then to find out what they were interested in and slipstreaming along with them to complement their offering without challenging it.'

Victor Newman

'Finding new people to connect with is not difficult, developing the relationship is harder and time consuming, so selectivity is essential for both parties. The best connection point is when you have something to base a relationship on.'

Donald Hudd

Build bridges

The hard reality is that network development means that you will probably have to walk up and talk to people you don't know and who don't know you. This means that you have to develop the ability to approach any stranger anywhere at any time and start a conversation. Even more, to turn this conversation into the start of a potential relationship where you might wish to develop a working or social connection.

Some people can do this effortlessly. They can hook and engage people with the quick-witted response, well-planned joke or insightful political comment. Me – I suck. I just find this so hard, as I suspect do a lot of other people who really would like to network effectively. I am still trying to manage this problem and develop a range of engaging strategies that will allow me to step onto the relationship bridge and begin to move across it.

This chapter considers five aspects that might be considered when you plan to build a relationship with members of your network:

■ How do you understand someone else's world and use behaviours which make that person feel at ease?

■ How do you define the best personal promotion strategy?

■ How do you bring to the surface and manage the hidden blocks that prevent a network relationship from developing?

■ How can you use language as a tool to understand the underlying nature of a relationship and from this build a robust bridge?

■ What opening strategies can you use that will help people warm to you in the first 15 minutes?

See their world

■ Effective networkers are able to use limited data to rapidly map and understand how other people see the world.

■ Once understood they are able to adapt and flex their personal style to match and pace the natural behaviours presented by the other person.

Imagine that you walk into a large room full of people. This is it! This is your chance to make some really great contacts and provide the initial boost to your career. However, as you look around the room it seems to be a heaving mass of noise and energy that swamps you. As you struggle to make the first move, thoughts are buzzing around your head, just whom do you talk to first, what do you say and how can you present your best aspects? You are facing the classic problem, one that faces any 14-year-old boy or girl at the first school dance. Just how do you walk across the dance floor (normally in front of all your mates) and ask someone to dance? How do you stack the odds in your favour to ensure a 'yes' and reduce the chances of looking stupid in front of your friends? Just imagine the number of teenagers who probably wish they had the gene of 'instant attraction'!

> There is a natural phenomenon or attraction process that we all experience. This is a tendency to be attracted to those people who are like us.

There is a natural phenomenon or attraction process that we all experience. This is a tendency to be attracted to those people who are like us. Look in any high street on a Saturday afternoon and you will see the formation of natural tribes. The young children group together in the playing fields; the retired people sit in the park; and the shoppers actively go about their business trying to get the job completed so that they can get home to open a bottle of wine and light the barbecue. Now look closer at these groups. Where you have teenagers there will be natural tribal clustering around certain themes. We have seen various tribal groups emerge over time: Mods, Rockers, Punks, Grungers and so on. These groups provide a natural home for people who share a similar preference for certain types of lifestyle, fashion or music. The other thing these groups do is to make it easy to recognize from a distance people with a similar preference. There is an instant recognition of someone else's inclination by his/her dress code, and once recognized, the introductions become easier because of the common maps. This can also be seen where people have distinctive cars as they merrily give a nod or wave to another driver even though they have never met them before. This implicit relationship helps to create a powerful emotional bridge with little effort on the part of either person.

In the same way, when you walk into this large room of people you have never met it can help to find ways to build strategies that help bridge the relationship. Now it might not be possible to identify people who share similar beliefs, values or hobbies as yourself purely by observation, but you can start to look for other behavioural clues that might help to bridge the relationship.

One way is to seek to map and measure other people's behavioural traits and use them as indicators to understand how they see the world. Once you understand their world maps, it becomes possible for you to match their language and ease the introductory process. When in Rome do as the Romans do!

Try to take each person as an individual and then understand his or her preferences. Once you understand their drivers, modify your language and behaviour to match theirs. For example, if they are loud and boisterous, then also be vociferous. If they have a quiet or reserved disposition, then match this when initiating a conversation. Alternatively, if the person is very logical, use rational language; if someone seems emotional, then try to be more affective in the language you use. By taking the time to understand the other person's orientation, the chances are that you will be better able to develop an initial sense of rapport with that individual.

> It might not be possible to identify people who share similar beliefs, values or hobbies as yourself purely by observation, but you can start to look for other behavioural clues that might help to bridge the relationship.

Let's go back to that room we entered which looks and feels like a heaving mass of bodies. Although people will have many preferences that drive their behaviour, there are two that can often be seen in the way people behave. These relate to how they use their 'personal space' and how they make 'personal choices'.

Personal space

As you look round the room, one of the first things that will stand out is that some people may be talking while others are listening. Take stock of what is happening and note those people engaged in conversation and those who are listening. Wait five minutes and take note again. After another 10 minutes take stock of who is talking. If the same people are still talking, then you might have your first behavioural clue.

This preference gives an indication of where people deploy their personal energy. Some people prefer to externalize things and in doing this create a field of energy that sits in the public space. Others prefer to hold their energy inside their private space and release it only when ready. For

Take stock of what is happening and note those people engaged in conversation and those who are listening. Wait five minutes and take note again. After another 10 minutes take stock of who is talking. If the same people are still talking, then you might have your first behavioural clue.

example, when faced with a new challenge some people will want to get some time alone to think through how they are going to approach the problem. Only once they are clear and focused on what they want to do will they talk their ideas through with other people. Other people will need to work the problems through in groups because they need the interaction, debate and group activity as a way to think things through.

The difference is that the first person gets his/her energy by being 'alone' and the process of spending time with a group of people can be quite draining. The other person prefers to be in a 'band' of people and gets his/her energy from the social interaction; the thought of being alone in a room for a while can be quite boring or limiting.

There are behavioural characteristics that go with these preferences (Table 5.1).

Table 5.1 Alone or in a band

Personal space	
Alone	*Band*
■ Will tend not to talk a lot	■ Will tend to talk a lot
■ Has a preference to work alone	■ Has a preference for meeting and working with people
■ Tends to think first and then talk	■ Tends to talk first and then think later

Personal choices

When you look further at people in the room and the language they are using, you might start to notice a difference in the words used regarding the decisions they take. Some people will seem to base their choices on facts, reality or hard principles. This type of person may have a preference to make decisions based on what appears to be logical or rational decisions. This is very much a Fact type decision-maker and can be seen to be quite sensible in the way he/she makes choices.

The other type of person will use emotional language and seem to be quite personal and affective in how he or she talks. These people will make decisions influenced by emotional criteria. They will focus on what feels right at that moment in time and are effectively making a heart choice.

The behaviours associated with these preferences can be seen in Table 5.2.

Table 5.2 Emotive or factual

Personal choices	
Emotions	*Facts*
■ Values based – i.e. this feels right for me	■ Principle based – i.e. this is the 'right' thing to do
■ Tendency to take decisions that strive for effective relationships and consensus	■ The need for a right decision may take precedence over the success of the relationship
■ Sensitive to the needs and emotions of others	■ Will assess pros and cons to put logical factors first

Now thinking about the two preference types, where would you place yourself on the scale in Figure 5.1. The important thing is that your placement is a natural preference and not where you always operate. Like a preference for being left or right handed, red or white wine or sleeping with the window open or closed. It doesn't mean that you cannot adopt other preferences, it is just your comfort zone, the place you would return to when the pressure is off and you want to feel comfortable.

Figure 5.1 Self-assessment scale

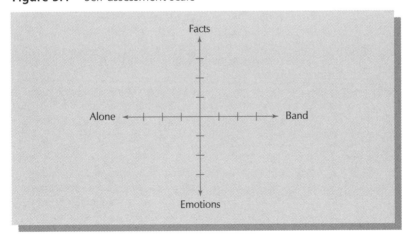

Bridge profile

Now we have four separate preferences that describe how people see the world. The next step is to bring these together into discrete units that describe in more detail how people might behave in a social setting.

Table 5.3 Rock, sage, star or judge?

Type	Description
Rock Alone Emotions	The Rock is seen as pleasant, steadfast and routed in a set of strong personal values, and often has a willingness to help others.
	The problem is that Rock people can be perceived as slow to adapt because their values will lock them into a certain place and they find it quite difficult to change. This slowness to change might also be perceived as stubbornness and the more you push, the harder they dig their heels in, even if what they are doing makes no logical sense to anyone but themselves. This can also be interpreted as a tendency to want to please themselves and not pay heed to others' deep needs. Much of this inner activity that they are processing is not apparent to others because they are focused on their own personal space.
Sage Alone Facts	The Sage is seen as a precise, conscientious person who has the ability to critically appraise something and draw strong conclusions on evidenced data. This gives the Sage the ability to take a perceived objective viewpoint and not be contaminated by emotional fog.
	However, others can see this objective approach as coldness, where the Sage forms his/her own conclusion and tends not to trust the views of others. The fact that Sage people need to do this on their own can make them appear aloof and remote and in many cases unresponsive to others. Also, because this objective standpoint is important to them they might silently judge others by their ability to follow the same process. Finally, the need to check the facts means that they can find rapid or unpredictable change difficult because they are internally trying to understand why it is happening.
Star Band Emotions	The Star has an amazing capacity to make friends, develop contacts and send out optimistic signals to the world. Stars wear their heart on their sleeve and boy do people know it. Because of the ability to externalize their feelings they are verbally effusive and good at selling their ideas.
	However, they might also be perceived as being inconsistent without real solid or objective information to back up their arguments. Because of this emotional value-based exterior they can be difficult to manage logically. They will tend to judge others by their matching ▶

level of empathic articulation and effervescent energy. When under pressure they can fall into a trap of being disorganized and careless, which is rapidly apparent because they will externalize their emotions.

Judge
Band
Facts

The Judge tends to be very effective at getting things done, and will do this by the externalization of logical energy that is grounded in solid facts and irrefutable arguments. This is the classic project manager who has the ability to get things done by force of argument and powerful persuasion.

The danger is that this power can be misunderstood. Such people can be seen as overdemanding, cold and critical. The desire to achieve the goals as agreed and the externalization of their energy can mean that any irritation they have of others can show through quickly. This is because they can tend to judge others by the same standard they apply to themselves, which is the ability to get things done.

These four network types can be mapped against the preferences seen in Figure 5.2. This is not to suggest that you can only be a Sage or a Judge. What this indicates is where your natural preference might be. Maybe your natural preferred style is to be a Rock, where you prefer to be alone and work on things that you feel passionate about. However, the reality is that we often have to operate in the other quadrants just to survive and pay the mortgage.

I was in this position a few years ago. My natural preference is the Rock as I like to spend time alone simply writing about things that I believe are important. However, while in the corporate stage of my career I was promoted into a new post as a pricing analyst. My role was to analyze, cri-

Figure 5.2   Network types

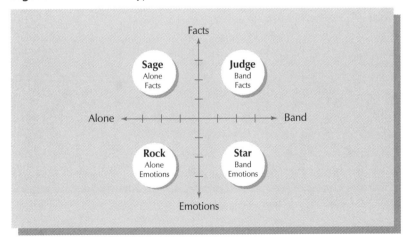

tique and comment on pricing strategies that were about to be presented to the main board which meant that I had to adopt the role of the Judge. This was quite a challenge on two counts. First, I had to go out and meet people all the time to talk about the proposals they were preparing and try to offer some support and advice. Second, the advice had to be logical and not of the emotional kind that I would prefer to offer. I did the job because I had to pay the mortgage and look after the family. But the important thing is that it wasn't my natural preference – I simply modified my behaviour to fit the role.

This is important because when networking we are not so interested in how people behave in relationship to their preferences. We are more interested in the interrelationship between the people when faced with each other. In particular, how one person can modify his or her natural preference in order to create an emotional bridge with people who have a different preference.

> When networking we are not so interested in how people behave in relationship to their preferences. We are more interested in the interrelationship between the people when faced with each other.

Hopefully you will have a good feel for your natural preference within the four types. The question now is what strategies can you employ to build bridges with the other three types. How can the Judge build a rapid relational bridge with the Sage or how can the Star make friends with the Rock?

Just imagine that a party is going on as seen in Figure 5.3. Four people walk into the room, one of each type. They each want to build bridges with the other three people but are conscious that they have a certain engagement style that means that sometimes things just don't click. The questions they each have to address are: What is my style? How will other people interpret what I do and say? How can I modify my natural preferences and so build a sense of rapport with each of the three people?

Figure 5.3   Bridging strategies

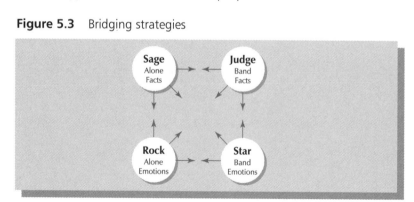

Table 5.4 Bridging from one type to the other three types

Your type	'Bridge-with' strategies	Their type
Sage Alone Facts	■ **Rock**. The Sage has a natural alignment with the Rock because of the shared 'Alone' preference. The primary area to focus on will be the Emotion orientation. The need in this case is to be more flexible in how you see things. Don't assume there is always a natural principle that makes things right – flex to respect the values of the person you are talking to.	**Rock** Alone Emotions
	■ **Judge**. The Facts preference is aligned with the Judge, so the area to focus on is the Band element or the Judge's desire to project his or her thoughts and feelings. Try to be more open about the factors and criteria that help you make decisions and be conscious of the fact that the Judge may say things without having thought them through as you tend to.	**Judge** Band Facts
	■ **Star**. The Star sits opposite both your natural preferences. You may need to externalize a lot more of your thoughts and feelings. Try not to judge Stars if they seem fuzzy, just value their passion and give them space to share these passions with you.	**Star** Band Emotions
Rock Alone Emotions	■ **Sage**. They share the same desire to be alone, so you will need to shift from an emotional decision-making style to a factual one. Try to slow down and be more precise and objective about things you say and questions you ask.	**Sage** Alone Facts
	■ **Judge**. Opposite on both counts so try to be more outgoing and use precise language that indicates the principles that guide your life. Listen carefully and you might hear some of the underlying principles the Judge uses to make decisions.	**Judge** Band Facts
	■ **Star**. You share the same emotional orientation so the emphasis should be on externalizing them. Talk about what you value and try not to let the Star's effervescence overcome or drain you.	**Star** Band Emotions ▶

	■ **Sage**. You share the same factual preference so the difference is in the fact that the Sage processes things internally while you project them. Be prepared to talk less and give Sages space to externalize their decision criteria.	**Sage** Alone Facts
Judge Band Facts	■ **Rock**. Dead opposite on both counts. Be careful that you don't beat them into the ground with your logical force of personality. Try to talk less and give them space to talk about their values – use more enquiry than advocacy.	**Rock** Alone Emotions
	■ **Star**. Here you share the same preference to externalize yourself, the difference is that they will push their values and you your principles. Be flexible and accept that what they say doesn't make sense – but understand that it is the right thing for them.	**Star** Band Emotions
	■ **Sage**. You are opposite on both counts. Try to stop talking so much and give them space to breathe. Accept that they might see life in black and white terms, whereas you see it as shades of grey.	**Sage** Alone Facts
Star Band and Emotions	■ **Rock**. You share the emotional preference but Rock types will keep it inside, whereas you tell people about it. There is little need to modify your language – just try to give them space – encourage them to talk about how they feel about things and don't cut them off mid flow because you suddenly want to say something important.	**Rock** Alone Emotions
	■ **Judge**. You share the same desire to externalize your energy but Judges will talk about right and wrong, and you might talk about maybes. Accept that they see black and white and don't try to convince them that life is built around people's needs and wants.	**Judge** Band Facts

The important thing with bridge building is the fact that you are willing to step inside out:[4] the intent and desire to accept that other people have a different way of looking at the world from you and that you care enough to try to understand this world. This fact on its own can go a long way to building effective bridges because it shows that you care about the other person.

In an ideal world you could hope that people will step into your world and see it as you do – but the reality is that this is not going to happen. As a result, if you want to build a network that is rich and diverse, then the onus is on you to develop the capability to see the world as others do and maybe adopt their behaviours just to make them feel at home when they step into your world.

Knowing you – selling me

- In any new network moment where you seek to build a bridge, you are selling yourself. The key is to understand what sales strategy will help you create the connection.

- 'Everyone is in business for himself, for he is selling his services, labour or ideas. Until one realizes that this is true he will not take conscious charge of his life and will always be looking outside himself for guidance.'   *Sidney Madwed*

When approaching someone with the desire to create a network relationship you are selling yourself. You are trying to promote yourself to this other person and ideally you would like that person to buy you or the ideas you are offering. In consequence, you need to have a clear sales strategy.

Two key factors that impact upon the success of the opening stage of a sales relationship are:

1. To what extent do I know the person (Known or Unknown)?
2. To what extent will the person have an interest in what I am selling? Will I have to press him or her to take an interest or has the person approached me (Push or Pull)?

By understanding where you sit against these dynamics it becomes easier to understand the nature of the sales relationship you are about to embark upon.

Figure 5.4   Known/unknown; push/pull

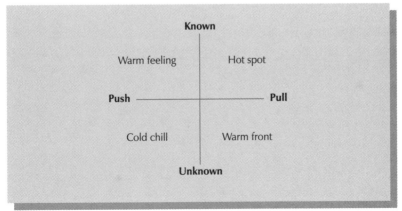

If we take the model seen in Figure 5.4, then our relationships will sit in one of the four quadrants.

- **Cold chill**. This is the tough one. You don't know the other person (Unknown) and the pressure is on to sell you or your idea (Push).

- **Warm feeling**. Life gets a bit easier here because you already have some form of relationship with the person (Known) but he or she will not have an obvious interest in the idea you want to propose (Push).

- **Warm front**. This is the alternate position. In this quadrant you know that the person is really keen on getting information/ideas similar to yours (Pull), but unfortunately you don't know the individual personally (Unknown).

- **Hot spot**. This is the mother lode. You have a relationship with the person already (Known) and he/she has an interest in the field you want to discuss (Pull).

Although there are clearly many ways to open up a bridging process, it often comes down to a choice of two core entry strategies, socialization or specialization, as seen in Figure 5.5.

For example, as you drop your child off to playschool you suddenly see someone that you have been dying to touch base with. You understand that she has terrific contacts in the government and you have an idea that you want to get in front of someone with influence in the government. You are at one end of the room and she is at the other. Somehow or other you need to build a bridge across the chasm.

If you decide to use the socialization style, the approach will be to promote yourself by focusing on the relationship rather than the idea. So you decide to use conversations focused on the person and not what she does

Figure 5.5 Specialization or socialization strategy

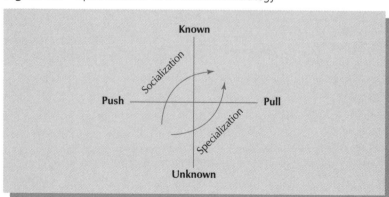

for a living. Clearly, here an opening conversation around the children is an ideal reference point. In other situations it might be the football match from the night before, holidays or hobbies or any general non-contentious topic that eases the flow of conversation and allows you to understand the person and to give him or her a chance to get to know you. Once this opening bridge is built, you will have an opportunity to make your pitch.

The alternative strategy is the specialization approach. Here your opening gambit is to build on the individual's interest in the topic that you want to talk about. Again, in this case if you know that the person is quite open about her contacts and is always happy to broker relationships, then entry through the specialization route will seem quite natural. Once you have been able to talk about your shared interests, the social relationship can in turn develop over time.

Ultimately there is no right entry strategy because people are people and they can react so unpredictably. However, by taking the time to understand the context before brooking the introduction, then the odds might be in your favour to pick a strategy that has some chance of success. At worst, if it is all going wrong, then maybe shift from socialization to specialization or vice versa – what can you lose?

The important thing will be your ability to switch between the strategies. In Figure 5.6 the route taken from the cold chill to the hot spot is quite a complicated one. The first move is socialization; this might be the time you meet someone for a coffee to catch up on things. After this you send him/her a copy of a paper you have written on a new product that gets you to point (b). From this the person is suitably impressed with your ideas and you arrange to meet for lunch one day to talk over the areas of common interest (c). You then send a proposition on how your new idea fits with the work the person is doing

> If you decide to use the socialization style, the approach will be to promote yourself by focusing on the relationship rather than on the idea being sold. So you decide to create conversations focused on the person and not what she does for a living.

> The alternative strategy is the specialization approach. Here your opening gambit is to build on the individual's interest in the topic that you want to talk about. Once you have been able to talk about your shared interests, the social relationship can in turn develop over time.

(d). You meet again for dinner and really start to focus on what areas of commercial interest you share (e), and then you reach point (F) where you both agree to cross-promote each other's products and ideas in the market.

This framework attempts to demystify the networking strategy that we all follow from the age of five as we seek to win friends and favour with children in the school playground with a combination of rude jokes and jelly beans. There is no rocket science with this approach, but it might help to make clear or codify much of what you do already. Once understood it allows you to manage the process more consciously and then enhance the biased entry strategies you already employ.

Figure 5.6 Building strategies

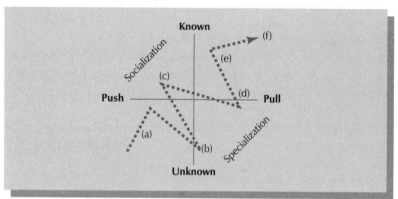

See the shadows

- What you don't say will often have more of an impact than what you do say in any relationship.

- The effective networker brings to the surface the significant shadows and buries the insignificant ones.

Shadows are one of the great unspoken problems associated with the idea of networking. They can bring a relationship to a grinding halt. No matter how much time, energy and money you invest in building bridges with someone, unless both of you are prepared to share that hidden thought or feeling, little social capital will be created.

A definition of shadow factors in relationships might be all the important information that does not get identified, discussed and managed in the open. The shadow side deals with the covert, the undiscussed, the undiscussible and the unmentionable.[5] These sit in the shade of the person and only appear when a light is deliberately shone upon them.

We might see this with the smile of a clown. The public sees the fool who entertains the children. But the glad expression can give the wrong impression because he or she is feeling sad.

> No matter how much time, energy and money you invest in building bridges with someone, unless both of you are prepared to share that hidden thought or feeling, little social capital will be created.

Shadows often exist in networks because people try to protect themselves from emotional pain. People make the choice to talk about things that will allow them to look favourable rather than surfacing issues that might lead to confrontation and upheaval. This is similar to the coping mechanisms that people in the emergency services develop to protect themselves from emotional pain. If one considers the emotional anxiety and stress that these people go through every day, they clearly have to develop the ability to separate themselves from the emotional pain and operate in a detached position. In the same way, people develop the capability to disassociate themselves from the bad news that starts to emerge if problems develop within a network relationship.

> Shadows often exist in networks because people try to protect themselves from emotional pain. People make the choice to talk about things that will allow them to look favourable rather than surfacing issues that might lead to confrontation and upheaval.

However, being aware of the shadows within a relationship and moving them to the surface is a different matter. Often our immune system becomes highly effective in resisting bad news and in many cases we chastise any individual who tries to bring it to the surface. The act of making the undiscussible discussible can be seen as painful, difficult, and in many cases downright threatening.

Figure 5.7 Surface/shadow split in an organization

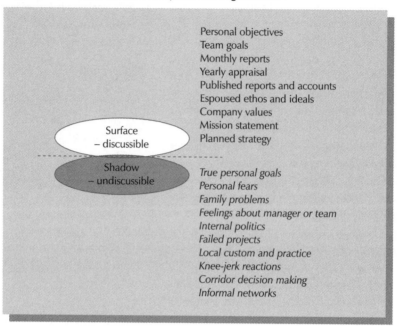

Personal objectives
Team goals
Monthly reports
Yearly appraisal
Published reports and accounts
Espoused ethos and ideals
Company values
Mission statement
Planned strategy

Surface
– discussible

Shadow
– undiscussible

True personal goals
Personal fears
Family problems
Feelings about manager or team
Internal politics
Failed projects
Local custom and practice
Knee-jerk reactions
Corridor decision making
Informal networks

Surfacing strategies

If you really want your network to be successful and sustainable, then it is important to spend time and energy managing the shadows. Although the emotional act of making the undiscussible discussible can be hard, there are simple strategies that you can employ to help manage this process.

■ **Disclosure**. This is possibly one of the most powerful and effective ways to open up the shadow area. If you are with someone who really doesn't want to open up (and we all generally know this when it is happening to us), be brave and open up to him or her. Find things that maybe you weren't going to share and explain that it is quite a deep feeling but that you want to share it so as to help the relationship develop. The benefit is that by sharing this and demonstrating that you trust the person, he/she might reciprocate and begin to open up. The problem is that the person may simply soak up all your shadow stuff and give nothing back. Only you can decide how far to go with this, but if you feel that nothing is being reciprocated, then in many cases it might be prudent to pull back for a while and try an alternative strategy.

- **Deflection**. This is a displacement process that is often used in marketing. Imagine you are walking down the street and a market researcher enquires whether he can ask some questions. He wants to test out a new perfume to find out whether people believe it will make them smell sexier. Now if someone sprays this on you and says, 'do you feel sexy?' – the chances are that it can be really awkward to answer truthfully because you feel embarrassed. However, if the researcher lets you smell the perfume and then shows the picture of a woman who is wearing the scent, you are more likely to answer the question: 'do you think that this scent will make her smell sexier?'. This is because the focus of attention has been displaced. It has created a safe haven where you feel that you can answer truthfully without being embarrassed. In the same way, if you are with someone who is showing signs of shadows, then talk about another friend of yours who has a problem he will not share with anyone. Talk about this and say that you really want to help him but are not sure of the best way to do it. Alternatively, maybe talk about a TV show or film that you saw recently where the characters caused all kinds of problems for themselves simply because they didn't open up when it was important. By virtue of making the shadows discussible, it may create a safe house for your friend to start to surface some of their issues.

- **Direct**. If your relationship is strong enough, then sometimes you just have to tell it as you see it. Maybe there isn't time to pussyfoot around or someone else is being hurt or damaged because of the shadow games and you just have to go for it. I had this with someone who had a drink problem. We both spent years avoiding the issue and just finding ways not to talk about it, until one day I surfaced the issue and said how I felt. It didn't resolve the issue directly (as you wouldn't expect it to) but it has certainly put it on the table now so that we can raise it again without having to play too many games.

- **Drink**. What can I say – you can use liberal amounts of alcohol to break down the barriers? It happens every night in most city centres after work and guess what – it often works! However, the down side is obviously that maybe just too many shadows can surface which leads to even more shadows the following morning when you meet the person and realize that you said things that shouldn't have been said – or even worse, you passed on other people's private shadows that were shared with you in confidence. In summary – big gain – but big risk.

- **Diversion**. Sometimes it helps to talk about something that takes the other person's mind off the shadow area and once the rapport is developed, you can gently ease back into the area without appearing confrontational. This way the bond and trust are put in place to ensure that when the shadows are surfaced the other person will not feel too uncomfortable.

- **Delay**. Sometimes it is best to not deal with it there and then. Just wait and bide your time until a convenient moment arises when it is appropriate. Just be sure that this is a conscious strategy and not natural tendency to avoid talking about something that may provoke an emotional response from the other person.

As with all bridging strategies, the objective is to create an emotional connection that will in turn allow you to develop a sustainable and successful relationship. The danger with these types of strategies is that they can be viewed and used as manipulative tools. This is a dangerous game to play and one that is diametrically opposite to the desire to create networks built on the model of shared success. My advice is to use the strategies if they help to build effective relationships. But always be open about the use of the strategy and never try to use it in a covert or duplicitous way.

Listen to the language

- The way something is said rather than what is said can indicate where you are on the relationship bridge.
- 'No one has a finer command of language than the person who keeps his mouth shut.'

Sam Rayburn

What is the one thing that drives your personal effectiveness in any relationship – be it when you are at home, at work or at play? It is generally your ability to manage productive conversations. If you are with your manager, child, or a friend in a bar, unless you can create and maintain a natural conversation, your chance of building an emotional bridge with the person will be limited. However, when was the last time you thought about how effective your conversational skills are?

The language or conversation between two people has a rhythm, groove or tone that we often feel rather than hear. We can emotionally sense if the conversation is aimless and going nowhere; if we are both avoiding a sensitive topic; if we are moving towards opposing views; if we are in general agreement about something; and when magic is happening and ideas and new thoughts are popping out every few minutes. It is often this flow of conversation that indicates the extent to which we are building an emotional bridge.

One way to do this is to listen to the tone and pattern of the conversation. For example, imagine that you are at a party. You are wandering around the room, just generally tuning into different conversations and listening to how things are being said rather than what is being said. Some conversations might seem surreal, where both people are frantically talking to each other without listening to what the other person is saying; some might appear to be aimlessly going nowhere, just choosing to talk about stuff, with each person tolerating the other person until something better comes along; you might hear some heated debate where the players are just verbally sparring and preparing themselves for the real fighting match once they have had a few more glasses of chardonnay; you might hear one or two where the players are actually listening and sharing ideas; and finally, if you are really lucky, you might hear a conversation where the people are really listening to each other and then sharing their thoughts, to the point that they are making the connections count.

> What is the one thing that drives your personal effectiveness in any relationship – be it when you are at home, at work or at play? It is generally your ability to manage productive conversations.

This limited selection of conversational patterns indicates the different type of interaction that can occur between two people. The five examples given above can be seen in more detail below as a set of conversational styles that we all tend to experience at one time or another:

- **Passive interaction**. In this case the debate between two or more people is happening without any real sharing of mindset. Each person might be talking at the other person and not taking the time to listen to his/her views and ideas. As such, each retains the existing map without increasing his or her own understanding. Examples of this can often be seen in political debate, where each person is there simply to put across a view, and not to listen to any opposing views.

Figure 5.8
Passive interaction

■ **Deflected interaction**. In some cases both parties can have a similar focus, but the idea under consideration is outside their respective personal maps, and emerging conversation can be seen as idle or superficial. Both individuals can be apparently engaged but there is little openness or debate around personal issues. Examples of this will be seen in the gentle conversation that takes place in a bar, or at the start of parties. Polite articulation is taking place but no depth of exposure or feedback is apparent. Both choose to focus on a topic that is safe and will not cause any discomfort.

Figure 5.9
Deflected interaction

■ **Locked interaction**. This is where people are at odds with each other. They are not just failing to listen to others, they are diametrically opposed to the other's ideas and thoughts. As such, the process of sharing moves people further apart, rather than bringing their maps together. Examples might be rival football team supporters: their love of a team blinds them to the acceptance of anyone else's viewpoint, and they are unable to step into another person's shoes to experience a different point of view.

Figure 5.10
Locked interaction

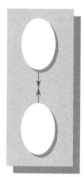

■ **Additive interaction**. A more positive viewpoint is where people share their personal maps of the world and as a result each person is able to augment his/her knowledge. In this case the process is one of a simple bidirectional exchange of ideas with little amplification taking place. This might be seen in the discussion at a team meeting where people share problems they have experienced and resolved them. Although knowledge is shared with the rest of the team, there is little amplification of the ideas and no new knowledge is generated.

Figure 5.11
Additive interaction

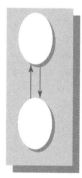

■ **Compound interaction**. The optimum level of interaction might be where the communication between a group of people results in synergistic outcomes and the amplification of people's ideas. As people expose their thoughts, ideas and personal maps, so the level of understanding and knowledge within the room will expand. Examples of this might be found in scenario planning workshops, where the interaction between people will ideally create new ideas, themes and patterns that might not have existed prior to the start of the conversation.

Figure 5.12
Compound interaction

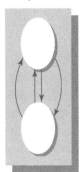

You should aim to be aware of your conversation style, what conversational style the other person is using and what style you would like to achieve. As you learn to rapidly map and manage the patterns, so you will find it easier to slip into high-value conversations that will in turn help to bridge the relationship.

For example, if you inadvertently slip into the passive or deflected conversational pattern, try to step out of that particular groove and instigate a new conversation. Gently close down the current stream and try to go into enquiry mode. Ask questions about the other person and as far as possible try to understand his or her world and personal maps. Once you understand how the person sees the world, it becomes easier to find connection points. These are bridge points that you can both talk about with interest and passion and hopefully develop a generative conversational pattern that becomes engaging and creates value for you both.

For example, imagine that you meet someone for coffee. You have never met before and you have decided to get together on the recommendation of a joint friend. As might be expected, when you first meet, the conversation centres around the weather (PASSIVE). Once you sit down and start to talk, it may drift onto a topic that you both have shared

> If you inadvertently slip into the passive or deflected conversational pattern, try to step out of that particular groove and instigate a new conversation. Gently close down the current stream and try to go into enquiry mode. Ask questions about the other person and as far as possible try to understand his or her world and personal maps.

knowledge of, possibly your relationships with the friend (DEFLECTED). Often what can happen is a choice point can be encountered. Down one route you start to share your views on your area of expertise but find that you have quite opposing views. Maybe you believe in one political standpoint and he believes in another. The risk at this stage is that you step into opposite camps and become unable to extract yourself from a polarized position (LOCKED). However, maybe you recognize the nature of the conversation and how it might trigger a locked position so you shift your language to the supportive style. You start to focus more on enquiring into why he believes certain things rather than advocating your view. The other person welcomes your enquiry and reciprocates the behaviour. As such, you move into a conversational style that is more open and positive (ADDITIVE). The value derived from the additive style helps you to recognize the worth gained from creating a connection. You then shift from an enquiry model and develop a more advocative style and suggest that you work together. The other person responds positively as he values your suggestion and also offers his ideas of ways that you might be able to work together. At this point you have moved from a casual conversation to a compound interaction where you can both walk away from the engagement having created a new network connection.

Now clearly first-time engagements don't always work this way, but the purpose of the story is to indicate the role that conversational patterns have on the relationship process. You can't choose how the other person will feel and think about you, but you can have a major impact on the person's behaviour by careful management of your language. This can make all the difference between connections that do or don't count.

Be like-*able*

- It may be tough, but likeability is an important factor in any relationship.

- It is so important that you might need to understand how you can help others to like you!

I guess there is no easy way to say this, so here goes – people generally network with people they like. Robert Cialdini suggests that this factor is often used as a powerful sales tool.[6] For example, the Tupperware party, where people are gently eased into a position of buying from someone they know and like rather than a stranger. He suggests that there are several important factors which help create this sense of 'liking' in the other person. These include quite basic things such as the level of physical attractiveness, where the beautiful people do seem to have an edge in the world. Another one is a compliment – saying nice things to people often breaks down huge barriers. Familiarity is important because we like things that we know and feel comfortable with. Finally, the extent to which you share the same background, personality traits or lifestyle can have a major impact on the formation of a network relationship.

> People generally network with people they like.

The final one is quite important because it is about being 'like-minded'. The cold, hard reality is that as human beings we tend to develop long-term relationships with like-minded people who share similar goals, ideals or hobbies. This is why we have natural tribes that form around football teams, Harley-Davidson motorbikes or rock groups.

Now, although this is no great secret, is it something that you consciously think about when you try to network? Do you just launch into someone and just hope he or she likes you, or do you consciously try to think about this notion of being likeable and how you can swing the balance in your favour? Do you know what you can do in the opening five minutes to at least get the other person to give you some time, or do you blow it in the first five seconds by making a real gaff in the way you try to develop a sense of rapid rapport?

Trying to develop affinity and long-term rapport with people in this way might be viewed as deceitful and duplicitous. However, I am suggesting that the first few minutes in a conversation can influence how it will grow for the next few years. The opening 15 minutes in the promotion interview, or the time you are stuck in the lift with someone when it breaks down, can affect the rest of your career. By developing a set of opening interpersonal strategies you can help people to accept you and maybe invest more time to understand the value you might offer in the long run.

> What if you are not a particularly attractive person, don't know the person well enough to pay compliments (or believe it would be unethical), and don't share a common map of the world?

The problem is, how do you create a sense of being liked if you don't have some of the key traits mentioned? What if you are not a particularly attractive person, don't know the person well enough to pay compliments (or believe it would be unethical), and don't share a common map of the world? What strategies can you draw upon that will help you to build this early rapport without looking like a dodgy second-hand car dealer? What are the behavioural factors that can help to build the emotional bridge?

Being 'like-*able*'

Now it starts to get really difficult as we try to understand and maybe define the behavioural elements that drive 'likeability'. For example, think about the following people:

- your best friend at work;
- the neighbour who lives on your right;
- the neighbour who lives on your left;
- the person who serves you at your local coffee shop;
- your partner's brother or sister;
- your last boss;
- the person who serves at the local newsagent.

Now ask yourself, of these people, who do I like and who do I not like? Think about why you like the people you like and why you don't like the people you don't like. Difficult, isn't it?

> Certain traits will cause people to not be liked.

This whole idea of likeability is really woolly and fuzzy. However, it is hugely important when it comes to networking. You can have the right skills, tools, contacts and products, but in many cases if the person you are trying to network with doesn't like you, then you might have a brief affair (exchange cards, promise to call, loads of text messages and e-mails) but the chances are that little consummation of the network relationship will take place.

How many people do you know who have an instinctive knack for connecting with others? Very few of us are born with it. The rest of us need to learn it. A lot of the secret to building bridges with people can be found in the ability to be likeable. Some people call it warmth. Some call it charm. Some call it charisma. But whatever the name, it is a key component in creating connections.

Now I do believe that like love, likeability is in the eye of the beholder. It is chemistry that delivers a catalytic reaction that is always unique to the people involved in the relationship. I cannot for the life of me see why my kids like some of the people they do – but they do and that is their prerogative. So ultimately we can never lock the ability to be liked into a formulaic prescription. However, there are certain basic traits that often help to create a degree of opening rapport between two people who have never met before.

However, before I attempt to pull out of the hat a definition that drives the ability to be liked, let me suggest certain traits that, in the main, will cause people to not be liked:

- **Talks too much** – is more interested in telling you about his/her world rather than listening to yours.

- **Uninterested** – seems unable or unwilling to take any interest in your point of view.

- **Selfish** – is focused on achieving his/her goals and has little interest in helping you to achieve yours.

- **False** – seems to present a counterfeit face to the world and maybe transparently offers you false praise.

- **Apathetic** – is indifferent, uninterested in things and doesn't appear to have any real energy or passion to build an emotional bridge with you.

Maybe if you met someone like this you would not warm to this person or get an immediate sense of rapport. Maybe you can do business because he has a product, service or market that you need, but would you want to meet him again if it wasn't in a business or professional setting?

Now consider if you met someone with the following characteristics, would you be inclined to meet for coffee and not fake a meeting that you have to rush to?

- **Listen** – always takes time to listen to your perspective and thoughts before presenting his/her own.

- **Interest** – actively asks questions about your world, interests and areas of activity.

- **Kind** – thoughtful, benevolent and seeks to put the other person first, concerned about your needs before his or her own.

- **Engaging** – the social capability to create a relaxed atmosphere by ensuring that the other person is at ease and entertained.

- *Able* – and willing to authentically put these attributes into play and in doing so helps to build a rapid bridge.

The essence of the Like-*able* structure is that you should care enough about the person to try to effect a sense of rapport and in doing this give the person a chance not to have to worry about working to build a relationship with you.

This is not about faking sincerity – as people will always see through this, if not immediately then over time and the end result will be a lost or soured relationship. You must always be

> The essence of the likeable structure is that you should care enough about the person to try to effect a sense of rapport.

authentic, but the purpose of this stage is to turn up some of the natural attributes that can be eroded after lack of practice. Think about the first school prom when you wanted to find a date for the night. You would really work to build the relationship because it was important. I suggest that the same amount of effort and passion needs to be applied whenever you want to encourage someone to join your network.

In summary

Ask yourself:

- Do I try to understand the other person's world view (Rock, Judge, Star or Sage) and modify my behaviour accordingly?

- Do I understand the sales context? How well do I know the person, and is this a push or pull situation?

- Can I see any shadows – if not, what might they be and what strategies can I employ to move to the surface those that need to be addressed early on in the relationship?

- What strategies do I have to move to a compound conversation as smoothly as possible?

- Have I thought through my Like-*able* strategy to ensure that I present the best of me?

'My "conscious" networking started late. Looking back I was networking (I suppose reasonably successfully) from an unconscious point of view – I've always given out trust in the first instance leaving others to show me if it was justified or not and I believe this, coupled to an enthusiasm to get the job done, has helped me in my relationships with people.'

Kenny Whitson

'The best networks act like gestalts where the different members perform different functions for a wider whole (i.e. pick your network friends for what you can't do).'

Mike Moir

Chart the connections

So far we have considered two aspects. First is the notion that any sustainable and successful network relationship must be founded on an abundance mentality. Second, we must learn how to build network bridges by managing the emotional or personal aspects of a relationship. Once we have these foundations in place, the next point to consider is how to make sense of our professional network. How do we know what we have, what value it offers and what changes need to be made to optimize its value?

> From this you can start to derive a fairly accurate idea of how the connections can help turn your personal capital into social capital.

To do this we must consider how to chart the connections. This is charting with a clear purpose. Like the sailor who lives and dies on the quality of the charts he or she uses to traverse the ocean, professional networkers must know how to chart and maintain the currency of their network connections.

In the same way that your bank balance shows the current value of your financial capital, a network chart will indicate the value of your social capital. Such a chart doesn't give you the facts and figures of what the network is worth financially but it can give you an indication of the reach and depth or your network, and from this you can start to derive a fairly accurate idea of how the connections can help turn your personal capital into social capital.

This chapter will help to consider the following:

(a) how to develop a network topology that indicates the degree of closeness between people;

(b) how to map similarity parameters against each network connection;

(c) how to understand where the value will be derived in each of the network relationships;

(d) how to develop a topology that pulls a range of key factors into a single chart;

(e) how to incorporate the level of social abundance into the network topology.

Tie strength

■ **If all of your network nodes were friends you would have a great time but never make a living.**

One of the first things to consider when you map your network is the strength of the relationship that you have with people. The really strong link might be one where you have regular contact with someone, you tell him/her all the important things that happen in your life, and you tend to be there for each other no matter what other demands are placed on you. The really great thing about the strong tie is the fact that you can depend on that person. You know that no matter what happens, you would be able to meet him/her for a drink, dump all your worries and start to make sense of the world.

However, there can be a few down sides as well. We all face the constraints of time. With only 24 hours in the day we have to make difficult decisions about how to allocate the time. Part of this allocation process involves making a decision on whom to see. Now, imagine you have this amazingly strong tie with John, an old school friend that you have always kept in touch with. You meet at least every Friday night to catch up on the week and talk about some of the new dreams you are chasing. However, this regular tie can begin to limit or constrain you. It can prevent you from meeting other people to ask for help on ways to get a job in their company. Dilemma – what can you do? On one hand, the strong tie with John is really powerful and adds a lot of personal value to your life. But it constrains you, as Friday night might be the time when other people would want to meet up.

The alternative model is where you might have a range of people you meet on a Friday night. Maybe you have a network of 10 people with whom you tend to socialize regularly. In this case you have a number of weak ties with a diverse range of people. Each person is important, but the ties are not so strong that you couldn't break an engagement without hurting the other person's feelings too much. The up side of this arrangement is that you have a wider access to the market and to a range of people who might be able to help you change jobs. The down side is that none of the relationships is that strong or close that you could talk about your real fears concerning the job change. The emotional link with the weak tie is more superficial than the strong tie and as such you don't have anyone really close to confide in.

The strength of the weak ties in your network is that they act as boundary spanners that have a finger in many pies. Because they might sit in a number of networks, they are able to help you access the social capital from networks other than your own. For example, the strength of weak ties is crucial to the labour markets. Job seekers are more likely to first hear about the job they eventually secure through contacts or people they did not know well (i.e. weak ties).[7] The essence is that ideas can reach a larger number of people and traverse greater social distances when passed through weak ties rather than strong ties, thus they create opportunities across different and discrete social and functional groupings.[8]

There is no hard evidence that people who are weak ties in your network will always be boundary spanners who will help you bridge into other networks as seen in Figure 6.1. However, since more frequent and intense interactions are likely to occur with people in your network with whom you have a strong tie, the implicit suggestion is that where you have a weaker link with someone, he or she probably spends time with people in other networks.

Figure 6.1   Boundary spanners

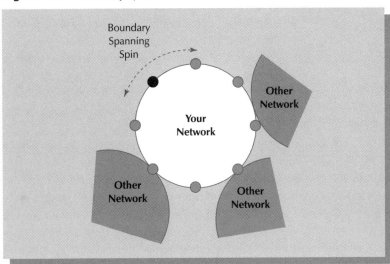

We should aspire to get strength from the development of weak ties. Because we can develop links to differing social networks and their associated social capital. This both broadens the range of our network and includes the possibility that we will be connecting with dissimilar people (more on this in the next section) who will bring a richer range of viewpoints into the network. Thus the creation of a heterogeneous network will probably offer a stronger social capital than the common homogeneous one that people often create for themselves.

However, there can be quite high risk in depending on boundary spanners as a resource to bring variety to your network. If they are the only link to the other network, you are dependent on their bridging contact. If this link is severed, then so is your access to resources or contacts in the other network. This gating process is an important one, especially in a career change. For example, the contact you have with a director in the department you want to move into gets transferred. The social value of that linkage is probably enormous and the work required to replicate that linkage might be so large as to make it untenable.

> Since more frequent and intense interactions are likely to occur with people in your network with whom you have a strong tie, the implicit suggestion is that where you have a weaker link with someone, he or she probably spends time with people in other networks.

However, the converse might be true if you are a weak tie in someone else's network. In this case you might want to initially maintain the exclusivity in order to heighten your extrinsic social value to the network! If your value to the network is in the access you offer to another group of people and this is currently your only value, then it might be in your interest to maintain your exclusive hold over the resources. Over time, once the network understands what additional value you can offer, you might choose to open up the market and give people access to your discrete area – but beware that you don't do it too quickly as you might be made socially redundant.

The first step in charting your connections is to develop a clear picture of the people in your network and where you would place them on this strong/weak tie continuum. Try to list the people in your network and set them out in a chart form as seen in Figure 6.2. Draw two circles and place those you have a strong tie with in the inner circle, and those where you might deem it as weak in the outer. Use the distance from the centre as a more specific measure of the strength of the tie if that helps. Also, where you have someone whom you believe is a boundary spanner who can bridge you into other networks, show that person on the edge and, if you can, indicate what other networks he/she belongs to.

Figure 6.2 Tie mapping

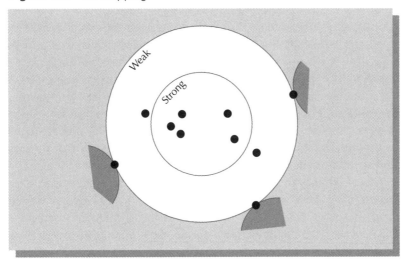

One might think that any effective net-worker will follow the mantra 'the more connections, the better'. However, this is not the case. What is true is that 'the smarter your connections, the better'. Social connectivity that provides the most benefit will come from links to connections you currently do not have access to. The goal is to be well connected to people who are well connected.

> Social connectivity that provides the most benefit will come from links to connections you currently do not have access to. The goal is to be well connected to people who are well connected.

Similarity

- Network strength comes from strong associations and network diversity comes from weak associations.
- Network optimization comes from a blend of the two types.

As a musician, my early years tended to be focused on networking with other musicians. This was because I liked being with people who shared the same interests. It made the conversation easy and the networking process was quite uncomplicated. This served a purpose because my focus and interest in those days was all around being a musician. Hence any growth in this network helped me to pursue my personal objective. We can see this in areas like football teams, the art world, political social clubs or anywhere

where groups of people meet with a shared interest. This is a homogeneous group that wants to be with people who are happy to be with them.

However, there can be a down side to such an inwardly focused network. The end result can be an incestuous group that develops 'group-think'. This is a concept identified by Irving Janis[9] where groups of people do not consider all alternatives, and they desire unanimity at the expense of quality decisions. These problems can be seen when closed networks develop a set of certain characteristics: not being critical of each other's ideas, not seeking outside viewpoints, and becoming highly selective in the people they choose to accept information from. The result is that the network can start to develop an unhealthy illusion of invulnerability.

As a result, they end up reinforcing a set of beliefs and ideas that make sense to them but are actually out of step with the outside world. We sometimes see this in the men's clubs and masonic-type institutions that come under attack from the press for being too much of a secret society. Even worse are the entrenched racial divisions that can be created as groups implode and focus on their needs and exclude those who are different. For example, in Robert Putnam's book *Bowling Alone* he shows how small-town Americans in the 1950s were deeply engaged in community life, but the social capital was inward focused and as such led to community and social division. During this period 50% of white Americans said that white and black children should go to separate schools.[10]

It is possible to prevent yourself from being too insular and closed within your chosen network by constantly exposing yourself to alien ideas. Make sure that you associate with people who are not the same, who don't have similar interests and who share beliefs and values that are not the same as yours. Specifically go out of your way to pull people with different perspectives into the network and try to import a broad range of non-related connections. Tom Peters talks about the need to associate every now and then with 'Freaks'. He suggests that you are as rich and diverse as the freaks that you spend time with.[11]

One example might be the analyst who works in the City, plays football at the weekend and spends one night a week at the local college teaching night school. This rich variety of contacts will ensure that the viewpoints never get too stale and open up a whole range of networking opportunities and areas that might not have been considered.

Open and dense networks

An open network is one where you are connected with people who are not connected with people you know, whereas a dense network is where all of your ties are connected to each other.

As a test – pick some people from your network at random. Write their names down and identify the extent to which those people know each other. If more than 70% of the group know each other, then you are moving towards a fairly dense network structure. Now look again – do those people have strong or weak ties with each other? If the tendency is towards strong ties, then you probably do have a dense network structure (especially if you have strong ties with a number of them). Finally, do those people in the group with strong ties and similar interests have certain normative rituals, sayings or private language? If so, then there is a good chance that you are a member of a network sect. This can feel really supportive and comfortable, but the contact link with people who are similar and have strong ties may not offer the rich variety that most people need to prosper and be successful over a long period.

There is also a good chance that people outside your closed group are experiencing one of two feelings. The first one is envy because they are also desperate for this type of close-knit community to help them feel loved. The second one is resentment because they feel rejected and excluded. This feeling will be compounded if for some reason they feel that you have rejected advances they have made to become a member. The risk is that this person might have power (surface or shadow) over your career and will set out to exclude you from his/her power base as a form of retaliation. This is one of the big risks with the formation of dense professional networks and ironically is a major force that fights against the whole purpose of the community because it can limit your access to certain people or communities.

This is why it is critical to include the levels of 'similarity' on your network chart. As part of your mapping process consider the chart you developed for the section on tie strength. Mark out those people who have similar interest as you with an A (for alike) and those with dissimilar interest with a D (for dissimilar). If someone falls in between, you can gradate the level to which they are alike or dissimilar, but for the first run of the charting process it is better to go for a black and white analysis and just mark people with an A or D. You can always go back to the data later to refine it.

You should now have a chart that looks something like Figure 6.3. This stage of the charting process will offer a first real feel for the make-up of your network. In particular, it should identify clusters of significance.

You might begin to see where you have strong ties with people in similar areas of interest and recognize that although this has strengths there is a danger of restricting your level of variety. You might see where you have strong ties with people in areas of dissimilar interests and begin to wonder how you can use this diverse reach as an opportunity to grow the richness of your social capital. Or you might start to notice how you have a broad number of weak ties in both the alike and dissimilar areas; this gives you

Figure 6.3 Network chart with ties and similarity mapped

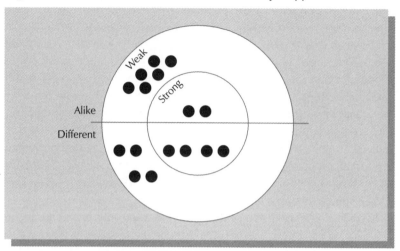

ample boundary spanners to call upon if you want to extend your reach into new networks.

Whatever the outcome, you should be getting a deeper insight into the nature and structure of your existing network. The next step is to consider why you are networking with the people listed. What is the payback for you both from the association?

Relational value

- Know if your connection is the person or the post.
- Know if your network value is who you are or what you do.

Always consider why you want certain people in your network (or why others want you). Is it because of who they are as individuals and their intrinsic value or because of what they do and the extrinsic value they bring to the network?

> The value of the social capital emerges from who you are rather than what you do.

Intrinsic social capital is where your perceived value is based upon personal capital that comes from within. It is something that you own and travels with you. This might be the behavioural skill of a lead guitarist, the ideas of an inventor or the emotional sensitivity of a great concierge.

With this type of personal capital people are attracted to your network and you are welcomed into theirs because of something that is inside you and has nothing to do with any role that you have in life or connections with other people. So the value of the social capital emerges from who you are rather than what you do.

Extrinsic social capital comes from the role you have in life or the people you know. It is a market value based upon factors attributable to you at the moment, but as a virtue of the role of office that you undertake. This can be commonly seen in the glamour, music and entertainment industries. People can be rocketed from nothingness to fame almost overnight, and all of a sudden find that they are in demand. If part of a rising boy band, they might be in the 'B list' of celebrities. After a number one hit and a fling with a famous star, they reach that pinnacle of success: the 'A list'.

> Extrinsic social capital can offer staggeringly high returns in the short run, but can plummet in value with the same speed that it ascended.

This extrinsic social capital can offer staggeringly high returns in the short run, but can plummet in value with the same speed that it ascended.

Just look at the ex-rock stars who are now plumbers, roofers and hamburger salesmen. The foolish people believe that the social capital ascribed to them has come as a result of their intrinsic capital. The wise ones understand that they have been handed a gift of short-term social worth and then use this treasure trove to enrich their inner capital. Consider the stars who started out as bit players and used this to step into a star role; from this they enhance their knowledge of the craft and move into a directorial or production role. This model can be seen in the music and sports worlds where the long-term players internalize the social capital and make it personal, and once personal use this enhanced value to augment their social value and so create an abundant and reinforcing growth cycle.

The question to ask yourself is, why do people ask to meet me? Is it because of who I am or what I do? Or ask yourself, what is it that I have of value to the world? Does it come with only me and is transportable wherever I am? Or it is something that someone else has conferred on me and which they can withdraw at any time? There is no definite rule of which is best as that depends on your journey in life, but it is imperative that you understand the source of your social capital.

One example of this can be seen in the thousands of people who take the big leap from being a full-time employee each year and throw themselves into a free agent or self-employed style of working. I meet so many people who assume they will get work outside the company because of the size and nature of contacts they have with their current role in the company. Wrong – big time.

The lesson for me when I made this shift was that when employed I could get speaking engagements more or less anywhere on the subject of my choice. However, once I left, none of the conference companies wanted to know me. Without the brand wrap of the company around me they were not interested. The hard reality was that they didn't really want me, they simply wanted to put the company brand on the front of the brochure so that it signalled that they were able to command speakers from blue-chip clients.

Maybe you need to ask the same question when you seek to embark on a relationship with others. Does their value come from who they are or what they do? It can be easy to confuse these two. The ramifications of not challenging this can cause embarrassment and wasted energy in the long run.

Taking the chart developed for the previous two sections indicate the value for the people in your network. For those people where the connection is in place because of who they are, mark an I. Where the connection is because of what they do, mark an E. You should get a diagram that looks something like Figure 6.4.

Figure 6.4 Chart with ties, similarity and value identified

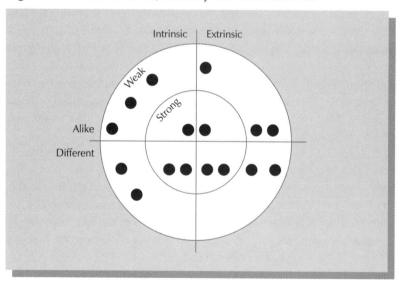

The chart is now blossoming with rich data. This information will help to bring to the surface the nature and possible value of your social capital and what areas you might focus on or change to be ready for the next career or life transition.

Network connection chart

■ Once charted, the connection chart will start to highlight holes and clusters in your professional network.

We have now mapped out the network connection chart as seen in Figure 6.5. This offers a structural map to indicate the shape and form of your professional network. This chart structure allows us to consider all the people in our professional network and map them against six different categories. Separately these categories indicate:

■ Strong/weak ties

■ Alike/different areas of interest

■ Intrinsic/extrinsic value.

When combined, it allows us to get a cohesive picture of the territory of our social capital. Where are the strong areas that offer us network strength? What are the gaps in the network, and importantly, what future action needs to be undertaken to optimize and grow the level and value of the social capital?

However, the map identifies only those people who are currently in your network, and if this process is to add value and achieve success, it is important to start to anticipate the future: to keep alert to the market and identify people who are not in your network but whom you might want to include some time in the future. By adding an outer wheel to the network chart you can quickly position anticipated network connections and place them in the chart, as seen in Figure 6.6.

Figure 6.5 Network connection chart

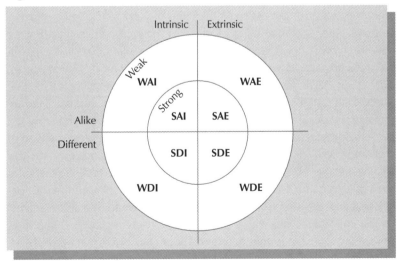

Figure 6.6 Target network

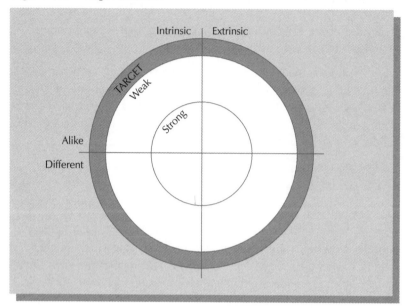

For example, you read in the paper that a local politician is lobbying government about a subject that you have a strong interest in. Although you don't know at present, you believe that there might be mutual gain in working together on this subject. So the quadrant where the politician would naturally go would be AE (alike, extrinsic), as you share similar fields is of interest and you want to build the bridge because of what the politician does rather than who he/she is.

Alternatively, you hear through your current network of someone who is highly regarded for professional ethics and the ability to give constructive feedback. The other interesting thing is that the person doesn't live in your country and visits only a few times each year. You are currently swamped with SAE network relationships (strong, alike, extrinsic), so much so that you are not getting any new and fresh ways of thinking and feeling. You decide that it would be really useful to create a WDI (weak, different, intrinsic) link with this person because it would help to richen your viewpoint and really get close to someone outside your comfort zone. Interestingly, the creation of such a network link can be quite difficult – because how do you know you will like people for themselves if you haven't met them? Maybe the initial strategy is to go for a WDE (weak; different, extrinsic) link with the anticipation that you move to WDI if you find that a sense of rapport builds over time.

The important thing with the network connection chart is that is does not seek to say what is right or wrong. It does not assert that one network topology is more effective than another or what your particular network configuration should be. What it does offer is a common platform to undertake a robust intellectual analysis of the current status of your network and start the design process to set out what it will need to look like in the future if you are going to be successful.

What the chart also offers is a way to categorize the various people in your network. This is categorization to aid understanding of the people in the network, not to lock down what type of relationship you have in a limiting way.

NCC types

The network type descriptor is made up of three core network factors. The first letter indicates the *nature of the tie*, the second the *similarity* and the third the *source of value in the relationship.* So someone you have categorized as 'SAE' (strong, alike, extrinsic) would be a person with whom you have a close link and share similar interests, and the relationship is based on what the individual does rather than on who he/she is. For example, this might be the middle manager in a large global organization who has a link with a manager in another country. Maybe they met at a conference, found they shared similar interests and have similar jobs. As a result, they decided to keep in touch and so hopefully help each other keep up to date with the latest corporate gossip.

> The network type descriptor is made up of three core network factors. The first letter indicates the *nature of the tie*, the second the *similarity* and the third the *source of value in the relationship.*

It is important to emphasize that the process of categorizing a relationship is second to the relationship itself. What the categorization does is to help the people step back and look at their network objectivity. If, for example, they were to step back and realize that all of their relationships were SAE, then they might be totally in touch with the politics of the company, but only at their level and functional group. They would not be getting information from other functional groups and, importantly, might be missing political data from other companies in the industry. To this end it might help to step back and understand the value in consciously and proactively developing casual relationships with people who work in other companies, and so build WDE-type relationships.

The network types identified by the network connection chart shown above are summarized in Table 6.1.

The final process in the design and management of the professional network is to carefully look at the various relationships and consider the level of abundance. There is little point in spending time and effort developing a range of great contacts in your company and industry to then operate from a squandered or subordinate position. If no value is being created or they are selfishly getting all the value, then you have to make some serious choices. Either ramp up the relationship to get to a shared or synergistic level or elect to back out of the relationship if you don't see a positive outcome.

Table 6.1 Network types

1. SAI   ***Strong, Alike, Intrinsic***. These are people with whom you have very close relationships and share similar interests. You also keep the closeness because of who they are rather than what they do. The stretch will be in the trust and tight bond between you. The down side might be a tendency to lock into a dependent relationship.
2. SAE   ***Strong, Alike, Extrinsic***. This is someone with whom you have a close relationship, possibly because you share similar interests. Much of the link comes from what the person does rather than who the person is. The positive aspect of this network relationship might be the ability to have a secure relationship with someone whose role can help you achieve your goals. The risk is that you place too much dependence on the person and that once his/her role or job changes, you are left high and dry. There might also be some disappointment on the part of the other party if he or she senses that you have dropped your interest in him/her after the role/job change.
3. SDI   ***Strong, Different, Intrinsic***. In this case, the relationship is a close one but with someone who has different personal or professional interest. The closeness might be driven by a desire that is based on the person rather than what he/she does for a living. The up side is a real opportunity to get insight into new areas and with someone you trust. One down side might be a temptation to get sucked away from your priorities. With a compelling relationship with this person you might find that less time and energy is being spent on the area where your core focus needs to be.
4. SDE   ***Strong, Different, Extrinsic***. This is a robust relationship with someone who has different interests from your own. It might also be that this bond is based on the person's role in life rather than anything about him/her as an individual. The value in this relationship might be found in the learning you get from someone who has knowledge in areas where you are weak. The possible problem might come if the person changes jobs. Is there any time left to hold the relationship

together or will it drift and fade? If the withdrawal is done with honour and integrity, then it is possible to leave the door ajar for future linkage, but if not, you might be seen as manipulative and duplicitous.

5. WAI   **_Weak, Alike, Intrinsic_**. This is a common relationship, one where you know and like someone with a shared interest but would not count yourself as close. This can be a very comfortable link and may offer a high-value low-maintenance link in your network. The one problem with this link can be the ease with which the 'Weak' can convert to 'Strong'. In isolation this is not a problem, but if you have a number of these links in your network, then it can be easy to get bogged down in networking rather than using the network to help create success.

6. WAE   **_Weak, Alike, Extrinsic_**. With this relationship, the connection is casual and with someone who has a role that is similar to yours. The benefit is that you can bridge very quickly with the person, even if you don't meet very often because of the shared interest. The possible risk can be if this person is a key boundary spanner for you and offers valuable access to other networks. If the person's job or extrinsic role changes, you might be exposed and unable to link into the person's areas.

7. WDI   **_Weak, Different, Intrinsic_**. This is the informal network link with someone you get on with personally who operates in a different area from yours. This is great because the foundation of the relationship is on the person rather than the profession, so the bridge will be robust even if you don't meet very often. Thus you have access to other work areas and networks via someone you trust and respect on a personal level.

8. WDE   **_Weak, Different, Extrinsic_**. In this case you have a casual connection with someone who might work in a different field from your own. The value is that you have linked with this person because of his/her specialist expertise and the possible help and advice that might be difficult to get elsewhere. The problem might surface if you get dependent on his/her expertise. Because the relationship is casual and only role based, you must assume that it has a finite life and be prepared to broaden your links in that area if you need access for a longer period.

9. TAI   **_Target, Alike, Intrinsic_**. This is someone in your field whom you would like to get closer to, maybe because you feel that there is the potential to develop a close personal relationship. The difficult thing with this is that you need to determine if the other person has a similar wish. The payback can be if the person would like to build a ▶

network link. The risk can be if you seem overly pushy and in doing so erode any chance of developing a relationship.

10. TAE *Target, Alike, Extrinsic*. This might be someone who is a friend of a friend in a similar work area to yours. You have met a couple of times and feel that the person can offer value to you by virtue of his/her role. The important thing with this build process is to clearly signal to the other person that you are interested in networking because of what the person does, not who the person is.

11. TDI *Target, Different, Intrinsic*. In this case you know of someone who operates in a different area and you would like to get to know the individual on a personal level and not just stick to the extrinsic type of relationship. This can be a hard bridge to cross because the person is in a different field and your goal is to focus on the person rather than his/her role.

12. TDE *Target, Different, Extrinsic*. In this case you have met someone who operates in a different field from yours and you would like to initiate a relationship because of the person's knowledge or role. The key issue is that although you might see value in what the person does, how can you help that person to see value in what you can offer in return?

Network abundance

■ Once charted, you can effectively tune the network.

■ Having a huge network that has little abundance is a pretty pointless exercise – maybe it is better to have a small one that overflows with abundance.

Networkers with an abundance mentality believe there are enough resources available to accomplish their goals. They also believe that their success doesn't mean failure for others. On the contrary, the more successful they are, the more others are affected in a positive way. They will regard success as something that emerges when both they and their connections are successful.

We can chart the level of network abundance by using the structure outlined in the 'Activate Abundance' section of the framework. The suggestion is that the nature of your relationship with someone can be thought of at five levels:

1. **squandered** – where little is happening in the relationship;

2. **subordinate** – value is being created, but you are not getting any of it;

3. **selfish** – value is being created, but all for you;

4. **shared** – you are both gaining value from the relationship, but it is additive rather than generative in nature;

5. **synergistic** – compound shared success, the combined effect is greater than the sum of the individual effects.

It now becomes possible to merge the abundance framework with the connection chart to develop a view of the actual and potential value of your social capital. The chart will then look something like Figure 6.7.

Figure 6.7 Network connection chart

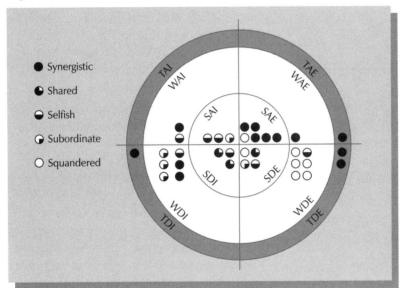

Collective network abundance is a difficult thing to manage but a fundamental tool that determines the long-term value and success of the network. There is little point in spending time and energy growing a personal network only to find that it produces less than the sum of its potential value. The goal with any network must be to help it exceed the value of the individual members. Unless the value of the social capital is greater than the sum of the personal capital, the energy being expended in managing the network might be better deployed elsewhere.

The things to look for as you seek to optimize the level of collective abundance across the network are:

■ **Things that trigger a scarcity mentality**. A scarcity mentality is something that few people want, but most people get it at some point in their career. It can be driven by both intrinsic and extrinsic factors. Intrinsic reasons can be from the influence of a few corrupt members who abuse the efforts of others, a general malaise in what the network seeks to achieve so people start to cash in their capital investment or shadow factors that cause people to believe untrue stories that are circulating. One important extrinsic factor is the sudden and unexpected economic downturn that triggers people to cash in and withdraw capital banked within the network.

■ **Identifying areas of low abundance**. Are there specific areas in the network that have a low abundance tendency? For example, do you have high abundance in the SDI sector but low abundance in the WDI? If so, is this because you are able to create abundance only with those you are close with, or have you developed high abundance in the SDI and less so in the SDE? Is that because you can only create high-value relationships with people where you treasure their intrinsic value?

> The goal with any network must be to help it exceed the value of the individual members. Unless the value of the social capital is greater than the sum of the personal capital, the energy being expended in managing the network might be better deployed elsewhere.

■ **How to spot a collective scarcity mentality**. It is easy to get caught in the trap of operating in networks that on the surface have an abundant approach but underneath are driven by a scarcity model. The way to spot this is by the small things. Look out for small signs of distrust, a tendency in people to cover their backs, failure to give credit to others, not inviting colleagues to important meetings and a general unwillingness to share contacts that sit outside the core network.

■ **Ways to enhance collective abundance**. Developing an abundant relationship with one person can be difficult but possible. It can be a lot harder to intervene and facilitate a sense of collective abundance across the network. In the main this is because the whole essence of the network is that it is beyond your direct control. Hence, the interventions you can make will be at a softer level: maybe to ensure that the network has a clear sense of purpose, that constructive conflict and debate is actively encouraged, and that fear is not allowed – fear of sharing ideas, fear of sharing feelings and fear of being wrong.

At the heart of the desire and ability to achieve collective abundance within your network are three core attributes: faith, hope and charity.

■ **Faith**. It is difficult to believe in the benefits of personal networking without a belief in the value that social capital can bring. Although this can be a leap of faith, without the core belief, the goal of collective responsibility will be subject to abuse and decay. It would be foolish to believe that effective networking means that you will always have happy relationships with your connections. Emotions can be volatile. One day we may feel happy with those in our network and another day angry with them. This is where the faith in the power of networking and benefits of social capital come into play. Emotions mislead us and a belief in transitory emotions can cause us to make bad choices. A faith or belief in the power of collective abundance will act as an unwavering compass, a map that doesn't need to be redrawn. Confidence in social capital knows that 'all things work together for good for those who work for each other'. It trusts in the invisible hand that stays active on our behalf even when we are not around.

> A faith or belief in the power of collective abundance will act as an unwavering compass, a map that doesn't need to be redrawn.

- **Hope**. This might be defined as wishful thinking. In many ways it is an extension of faith into the future. Hope looks forward in anticipation of emergent roles that take people to what they want to be in the future. Importantly, the ideal hope is not one where people want to escape from who they are and what they have, rather it is like the transformation of a caterpillar into a butterfly, a natural personal transformation that follows as part of a developmental journey. The personal network is often a powerful mechanism that helps people be who they are and what they want to be. Without this future-looking dimension to the network it may well stagnate and wither, thus eroding any opportunity for growth in the personal and social capital of the members.

- **Charity**. This means more than helping those who cannot help themselves. Charity in the personal network is the conscious will to do good to and for others, whether they deserve it or not. Charity doesn't seek gratitude, but more opportunities for expression to help others achieve success in how they think, feel and behave. This is an important aspect of the charitable process. Charity within a network sits across three fronts. Heart actions mean being charitable to others emotionally by being sensitive to their personal needs, understanding if they don't have the same level of motivation as you, or respecting their desire for privacy and space. Head charity is about being open minded enough to respect the fact that others have differing views from you or trusting people enough to share new ideas and thoughts with them. Finally, hand charity might be a willingness to make time for people. This might be listening to them run through an important presentation, helping out if they are stuck for a childminder on the day of an important meeting or simply giving feedback when asked.

The important thing is that abundance starts in the hearts and minds of the networkers. The more they think and feel abundantly, the more abundance they will give and get. The more abundance this generates, the more success people get, their teams get, the company gets and ultimately so will society.

In summary

Ask yourself:

(a) Have I got the balance right between people that I have strong or very close ties with and those who might be counted as acquaintances?

(b) Have I got a varied mix of people in my network – from those who do the same as me through to those that I would never consider mixing with?

(c) Have I considered the extent to which I link with other people? Is it for who they are or what they do? Have I been honest with them and myself? Do I know why other people want to network with me?

(d) Do I have a feel for the type of people in my whole network and is there a bias for one type of person?

(e) Am I clear as to the real value both I and the other person are getting from a network relationship? Should I invest and enhance the value of the relationship or maybe back out and close the link down if it has no future?

'My belief is that "knowing" someone has less value than someone "knowing" you and that it is what you are known for that will count the most. For example, I regularly saw the chairman of our company in the fitness centre each morning – we said hello each time. Through that exchange I considered myself to know him but later found out, when I applied for a job in his office, that our shared interest in fitness counted for nothing. When interviewed, he knew my face but that was it. "What do you do?", he asked. He didn't know me at all.'

Roland Stainton-Williamson

Dare to be different

If you are planning to network seriously, then people must be able to remember who you are and how you can add value for them. To achieve this you need to ensure that you stand out in people's minds. We are talking about rapid self-promotion and this is not a process for shy, retiring introverts. If you want your network connections to sponsor and support you, they need to know what you offer and how it differs from everyone else in their network.

Sometimes it can pay to view yourself as a product in an open market. You might believe that you are different, interesting and generally someone the world would want to meet, but in reality you are just another cornflake packet on the long row of cornflake packets in the supermarket. There are lots of great people in your network; the question is, how can you create large amounts of interest in you and your ideas? What will make people listen to you rather than anyone else?

Try to sit back a bit and look at yourself from a detached point of view. How would you convey the essence of you to other people? How would you condense a description of you into a 60-second pitch? If you can't describe who you are and what you do in 60 seconds, then there is little chance that anyone will ever get time to listen. I dare you to try it – it is generally the people who are well versed in self-management and promotion who have the capability to really condense their huge ball of value into a vox pop. Most people will wither, clam up and feel too embarrassed to say how great they are, or talk and talk and then talk some more as they try to explain their value. This ability to simply describe you is a powerful tool within a network and one that has to be practised until it becomes almost second nature.

> If you can't describe who you are and what you do in 60 seconds, then there is little chance that anyone will ever get time to listen.

The key questions to consider about your network diversity are:

(a) How can I create a representation of who I am and what I stand for across the network?

(b) How can I ensure that there is only one of me in the network?

(c) How can I ensure that in marketing myself across the network I don't present a false representation of who I really am?

(d) How do I condense all of what I am and do into a simple representation that people will remember?

(e) How do I effectively promote myself in the network?

You and you alone

- **You must be unique within your network. There can only be one of you, and you must try to stick in your colleagues' minds. Your personal brand recognition needs to be instantaneous and sticky.**

Networking isn't a game for shrinking violets. If you are reacting adversely to any of the ideas on this page then beware. This is a game of self-promotion and you are in the Coke, Nike and Harley-Davidson business. Your goal is to create a tribe of people, a tribe that gets you, wants to buy a part of you and is proud to say it knows you.

Write one thing that makes you different in this world . . .

Now write another . . .

And another . . .

And finally . . .

Find it difficult? If so, don't be surprised as most people struggle with this. One of the great things about a democratic society is that it offers freedom to be who we are and what we want to be. The trouble is that most of us don't take the opportunity to find this. Instead, from an early age many of us are processed and packaged into being good little children our parents, teachers and masters want us to be. The talent that we are all born with becomes abused, moulded and reformed into something that is 'OK' rather than being something wonderful that can brighten the life of other people. Many of us are lucky enough to live in a world that offers freedom to 'be' but instead we choose to be what others want us to be. This is part of the dumbing-down process that begins from the age of five and probably continues until the age of 50. School, college, work, promotion, and so on act as lead weights that create an 'average level of mediocrity'.

Charles Handy, in his great book *The Elephant and the Flea,* talks about his school life. He left school convinced that the best way to survive was to find out what the rules are, keep your head down, pass the tests as best you can, and carry this on until death or retirement takes over.[12] He cites a wonderful piece by Pablo Casals that asks: 'Why don't we teach our children in school what they are? We should say to them "Do you know what you are? You are a marvel. You are unique. In all the world there is no other child exactly like

> Well, let me say it now – I believe that you are unique and there is no one else like you in the world. You are unique!

you".' How many times has that been said to you in your lifetime? Well, let me say it now – I believe that you are unique and there is no one else like you in the world. You are unique!

The challenge now is how to undo the years of vagueness, ambiguity and dumbing down and to help take away the blinds of restrictions to see just how singular you are. Tom Peters does a great job of this in his book *Brand You 50* when he says 'Your life is at stake here. So look at yourself and your skills/talents/potential . . . With brutal honesty. You probably have more (a lot more) to offer than you realize. So . . . '[13] It is the '*so* . . . ' element that I want to address here.

One way to open up your unique or singular gift is to map your personal capital. This might be described as all the ideas, feelings and skills that you have and are able to deploy that will create value in your chosen market. For plumbers, it is their ability to calm the worried homeowner, diagnose the problem and then repair the damage with minimum fuss; for musicians, it is knowledge of the chords to play, the ability to play the music correctly and with passion; for man-

> Personal capital might be described as all the ideas, feelings and skills that you have and are able to deploy that will create value in your chosen market.

aging directors, it is knowledge of the business and market, the capability to forge complex political relationships and the practical ability to physically lead others in times of crisis.

Personal capital

Your personal capital might be broken down and analyzed against two primary criteria. The first is the *currency* or the capability used to transact with the world. The second is the *stock* or how this currency is stored.

■ **Knowledge currency**. We acquire and offer knowledge to the market through one of three routes: cognitive (head), affective (heart) or behavioural (hand).

    – **Heart** is the emotional or affective capability we use within ourselves to manage our relationship with others. Daniel Goldman describes it as the inner rudder that guides our life, directing who we are and where we are going. It is the inner force that gives us the necessary strength to make choices and set clear goals that will not be swayed by the views of others.

    – **Head** is our cognitive ability and is often viewed as our intelligence or general mental ability. It refers to the capability of people to process information and to use such information to manage their behaviour.

    – **Hand** is a generic term covering behaviour, physical activity, responses, reactions, movements, operations, etc. In short, it is someone's observable behaviour or action.

Figure 7.1 The three routes of knowledge currency

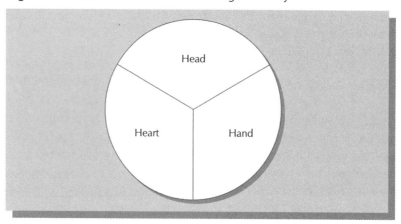

■ **Knowledge stock**. This refers to how knowledge is stored, in both tacit and explicit form.

    – **Explicit** knowledge is that which can be expressed in words and numbers and can be easily communicated and shared in the form of hard data, scientific formulae, codified procedures or universal principles. This is the hard and tangible knowledge that can be codified, replicated and readily transferred across an organization.

    – **Tacit** knowledge is the informal, hard-to-pin-down ability. It is in the fingertips or muscle capability – where people can perform a task, but find it difficult to explain. It can be the knowledge that you don't recognize that you have, e.g. how to open a door may not seem like 'knowledge' until you meet somebody who's never seen a door.

If we combine these two elements we arrive at six factors that make up our personal capital and are presented to the market as our talent as seen in Figure 7.2.

The talent wheel in Figure 7.2 indicates the bandwidth of your personal capital. There are six levels ranging from Explicit head through to Tacit heart. This bandwidth is taken to market in the form of your *personal talent* and this creates market value.

Figure 7.2 Talent wheel

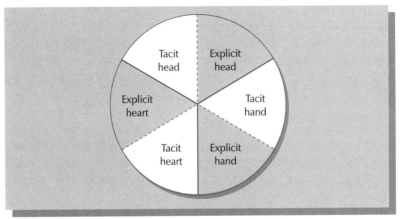

Everything we do when building or maintaining our network can be seen to flow through these six aspects of our personal capital. For example:

- **Explicit hand**. These are the behavioural strategies that you knowingly employ to build and manage your network. It might be the fact that you always seek to spend close time with people rather than just calling them on the phone.

- **Tacit hand**. These are the physical or behavioural patterns that we follow without thinking. It might be the fact that your palms sweat when you walk into a strange group of people; you have a great way to build rapport and trust with strangers; or you have a naturally charismatic style that makes people want to invite you into their network. The essence with this element is that you might know that you can create value using this capital but are not sure how you do it or can stop doing it.

- **Explicit head**. These are the maps, strategies and processes that I consciously and knowingly use to manage my world. It might be who the key people are in my field, business strategies or books and ideas.

- **Tacit head**. This is the unspoken and often unknown assumption or maps that we use to manage ourselves and others. This might be who is 'in' and 'out' at any moment in time. Without consciously realizing it I often notice that I am spending more time with certain people or associating with certain groups while other groups have faded into the background. This hasn't been a conscious thing, it is just a gradual remapping over time. Only by becoming more conscious of this tacit remapping process that can occur can I ensure that I don't lose contact with people with whom a large stock of social capital can be generated.

- **Explicit heart**. These are the known emotional strategies that we use to motivate ourselves and build relationships with others. It might be the little mantras that are repeated inside or a well-practised phrase or joke that will help break the ice.

- **Tacit heart**. The tacit heart factor is the inner security that gives us the confidence to be who we are and not worry about what other people may say or think about us.

This is essentially the bandwidth or spectrum that you present to the network (and your market). It is really important that you understand what you are offering for each of the six layers and tune the presentation accordingly.[14] For example, do others value your explicit ideas and thoughts? Do they value you for your deep, tacit appreciation of a particular market? Do they call upon you because you have certain physical skills and behaviour that you can employ with the team? Do they feel that your strength is in your tacit negotiation skills? Is part of your appeal the emotional techniques that you use when making a presentation in front of a large audience, or is your strength the fact that you have strong inner security that allows you to really challenge clients in pressure situations?

As you attempt to differentiate yourself with the network, one way is to use the talent wheel and ask yourself: what do I do in each of the six layers? Where are my unique skills? In what area am I seen as a commodity? What can I do to enhance any of the important layers? For example, Table 7.1 shows the first cut that a consultant might make in mapping his or her talent wheel in defining what he or she offers against each of the six segments.

Once the consultant has built the talent wheel, then he or she can make decisions on the areas that will offer the most differentiation. Much of this

Table 7.1 An example of talents analyzed by segments

Explicit hand	General consulting skills Specific functional or technical skills. Ability to produce reports/presentations, etc. Listening strategies Relational or rapport-building strategies
Tacit hand	Facilitation skills – putting people at ease Open/closed body language as necessary Doing the right thing at the right time Intuitive bridge building Kinaesthetic skills
Explicit head	Intervention/change frameworks Business organization Measurement techniques Industry/sector knowledge Diagnostic and clarification strategies Negotiation strategies Financial models Influencing/political strategies Decision-making tools Modelling frameworks Ethical criteria Information technology Case history/stories
Tacit head	Knowing when not to intervene Intuitive problem-solving approach Knowing when not to give the answer Give a sense of assurance that have seen it before Able to make intuitive links and synthesize Using the right language (social, political, organizational) Rules of thumb associated with previous experiences To know when to bluff and when to concede in negotiation Financial prudence Deep influencing patterns Intuitively identify the optimum choice Ethical choices and consequences Knowing what pricing strategy to employ ▶

Explicit heart	Espoused or stated values
	Customer relationships and strategies
	Sales techniques and strategies.
	Able to map the emotional needs of the moment
	Inner-security strategies – personal mantras
Tacit heart	Charisma that opens closed doors
	Self confidence or inner security
	To just 'know' when someone is faking it or lying
	Broad shoulders to take flack meant for the client
	Empathize with the clients' and consumers' pain during a change
	Independence and willingness to walk
	Values and integrity
	Socially responsible and a feeling for the right thing to do

will be driven by two factors: what can the consultant do better than other people in the network, and what is it that the network wants/needs/values? By understanding this, you can start to really define who you are and what you do that makes you different.

Think about your talents in each of the six dimensions. What capital do you have in these areas that helps you build and manage a network? Do you have talents that separate you from the pack? Do you have liabilities, i.e. things that you don't do well in any of the areas? If you don't have capital in any of the areas, can you trade with someone else to get it?

Unless you take the time to look inside and understand your personal capital and how you present this to the market, then your whole networking process may be flawed. If you don't have anything of interest for other people to want to network with you, the chances of getting a network up and running will be flawed to say the least!

If you are not too sure what your talent is, then get a few people whom you trust and ask them what they would praise you for. What would they tell others about you? What have they found that customers repeatedly want your help on? You will then start to get an indication of the 'deep you'. And that is where the uniqueness is to be found – so deep that no one else will be able to copy or replicate it because it is an essential part of who you are and what you can offer the network.

Bang the symbol

■ Make it easy for people to recall you and your personal brand.

In many cases your most important asset will be the intangible capital, your personality, identity, attitudes, success and social awareness. These social assets are effectively your personal brand equity within the network and are one of the primary tools that you will need to use to maintain your valued position in the group. Often it can help to find a way to condense and crystallize all these intangible assets under a tangible brand symbol. This is an easily recognizable and attributable mark or representation that everyone will know is indicative of you and the value you provide.

Consider the naming of cars after animals – Jaguar, Cougar, Mustang – what symbolism is being suggested with this representation? The image that these animals offer is not that akin to plodding on a journey from one town to another. Maybe they evoke a spirit of freedom, speed or supremacy. By creating a symbolic link with such animals, the manufacturer seeks to evoke a set of thoughts and feelings within the buying public.

What do consumer products have to do with our ability to differentiate ourselves in the network? The link is that we can all learn from the expertise that the consumer industry has acquired in its marketing campaigns. We drink Coke because it is the 'real thing', and we wear denim because its uniformity helps us to join a global tribe almost effortlessly, hence, the market success of a consumer product will be heavily dependent on its ability to lock the symbolism in the consumer's mind.

We are sensible people and your network members all behave in practical ways. However, although we might wear a shoes to keep our feet warm and dry, at a symbolic level of awareness we wear cowboy boots, for example, not because we rope cattle, but because it is symbolic of rugged individualism. Or, we wear sports trainers because we want to look athletic or sporty.[15] The challenge is to create a symbolic attachment that can entice and engage your members such that they want to associate with you and even more are really keen and proud to tell their friends about the great things that you do.

The advantages of creating a symbolic wrap around your brand include the following:

■ As the network grows above a certain size, names can become blurred, and when your name becomes blurred – so do you. By use of a symbol you can lock yourself in the mind of your network audience and so ease the recall process.

- A symbol will provide cohesion and structure to what might be a complex set of product offerings, in the way that a confectionery or car company will use the superordinate brand symbol to sit on top of a range of complex offerings.

- It facilitates the tangible communication of intangible value. Think about the one product that you really love. It might be a car, audio system or clothes range. You may love it to death but can you explain why – it becomes really difficult to communicate what can be tacit heart or emotional factors in an explicit way. However, the use of the brand symbol will do it all. For me, I will walk past a whole range of coffee shops just to hunt for the Starbucks logo because it just feels right when I walk in the door – laptop in hand ready to crash with a hot cup of tea.

- It facilitates a more effective decision-making process. Ultimately you are in a network because you want help from people. This means that they will have to make choices – the next time you put a call out for help, they have to choose to help you or to help someone else in their network who needs some information or support. Personal support doesn't come in a bottomless bucket and sometimes we have to say no to network members, because we are too busy. By planting a clear symbol of who you are and what you stand for in the minds of your peer members, there is a greater chance that they will be able to make an effective decision because they clearly understand who you are, what you do and maybe how you can reciprocate in the future when they need help.

- It provides a strategic-level position while your products and services can flex with the market needs. If you think of some of the great brands and logos, very often the products and services a company supplies will change over time. This doesn't matter because often what people trust is the symbolic nature of the brand or logo rather than really understanding the full product set being offered by the business. In the same way, the product set you offer to the market will probably change over the next three years. However, if you have your symbol in place, it will provide continuity and peer trust at a surface level, leaving you free to flex underneath without having to really let your network know in details what changes you are making.

Kevin Roberts, CEO, Saatchi & Saatchi suggests that a trustmark is a distinctive name or symbol that emotionally binds a company with the desires and aspirations of its customers. It's the emotional connection that lets you go out and conquer the world![16] The key point that we will get to later is that the whole essence of networking is built on the idea of trust-based connections. Your symbol is essentially your trustmark. Whereas companies will use trademarks to protect their intellectual capital, as a networker you need to protect your social capital and your selected symbol is the signal and representation of the trust that you have in the network.

> Your symbol is essentially your trustmark.

Find it – don't fake it

- 'Those are my principles, and if you don't like them . . . well, I have others.'
  Groucho Marx

- You can't sell what you don't have.

Sincerity is the desire and ability to be open and truthful and not deceitful or hypocritical. It is essentially the art of being authentic: being who you are with everyone you meet, and doing this from a position of strength. My suggestion is that within a network you have very little choice but to be sincere and authentic. You might get away with falsifying your market pitch for a short period but ultimately you will be found out and the chance is that the network will collapse around you – probably in a matter of days.

People are at their best when they are themselves, not when they are forced to put on a veneer of pretence about a range of expectations that others have decided they need to project in order to 'live the brand'. 'Be yourself' will often be a more inspiring and triumphant model for positioning oneself in a network than 'be the brand'.[17]

By accepting that your professional network brand is based on authenticity, you are either digging a big hole for yourself or creating a huge mountain. Volvo can't claim to build safe cars and then build dangerous ones; Apple can't promote it's innovation capability and then be second to market; and Durex can't sell itself as a safe contraceptive company if it is letting the little buggers through by the thousands.

To market yourself with sincerity is quite simply using nothing but the truth every time you touch another person. Think about how you felt the last time you met someone at a party who to you seemed really impressive, but then heard later from the host that a lot of his personal pitch is actually bluff with little substance underneath. Like the books or junk mail messages that boast *'We will make you a millionaire in a year'*, you immediately know it is a scam and don't even reply or show any interest.

I once had a cold call from a guy trying to sell me a training programme so I gave him a couple of minutes to make his pitch. Half way through I started to chuckle to myself. The course he was trying to sell was a programme on how to sell yourself over the phone – the trouble was that he was awful. He didn't do any of the things that he said his course would deliver. Now, I don't blame him for trying to make a living, but the trouble was that he was not being authentic with himself or me as a potential customer. There was a basic disconnect between what he said he could do and the evidence of what he really did. As a consequence, he spoiled his chance of building a relationship with me and in reality spoiled the chance of making a future sale. Once people spot the lack of authenticity, it is a hard hill to climb back up again.

The two simple rules for personal brand sincerity might be:

1. Tell the truth to your network.

2. Your product or service should do what you say it does.

People know when someone is faking it, so always ensure that your brand positioning in the network is true to your beliefs and values. If it is not authentic, you risk looking duplicitous to those who really know you!

Simply simple

■ 'Making the simple complicated is commonplace; making the complicated simple, awesomely simple, that's creativity.'

Charles Mingus

■ 'Everything should be made as simple as possible, but not simpler.'

Albert Einstein

Look in your free newspaper under the trades adverts. One of the differentiating things that always stand out for me is how advertisers present their talent. Some will advertise themselves as a master builder; list their specialities, qualifications and maybe how many years they have been trading. Another type is the person who advertises as a builder, plumber, carpenter, gardener and odd-jobber. The sheer proliferation of identities is really confusing. I always question which of the listed talents they are good at and which they have thrown in to just pick up some cash when times are tight. Whereas with the first kind of advert you are very clear on what you are getting and the chances are that you will remember the associated brand, with the second one the brand has been cluttered up by the complexity of the presentation.

You are just one in a potentially large network of people. The question is how can you get this network to remember you. Peter Sealey, ex-Procter & Gamble and Coca-Cola, suggests that companies need to make simplicity a selling point. He cites BMW with the 3-series, the 5-series, and the 7-series. You know instinctively which is the entry-level car and which is the top of the line. You know that the 540 model has a more powerful engine than the 528.

Where would you position yourself in your network? Are you an entry-level player, do you have mid-range power and prestige or do you want to hit the network as a prestige model? You need to be absolutely clear both on where you authentically sit and then how you present that simple message to the network.

■ Don't make other people have to work to remember your brand.

■ Do make it easy for other people to deposit your brand in their memory bank.

■ Don't try to mix multiple messages in the one brand message.

■ Do give them hooks to hang your brand on through positive association.

Presenting yourself in a 'simple' way may look straightforward, but it isn't easy. Simplicity exposes the quality of an idea. Although the trend is often for people to over-think and over-produce, now is the time to simplify. Don't give your network peers a five-page CV – give them a one-paragraph statement that suggests how you can add value to their life and a one-paragraph statement that clearly sets out what you would like from them.

> Simplicity exposes the quality of an idea. Although the trend is often for people to over-think and over-produce, now is the time to simplify.

Instead of pushing too many choices on your network, try to concentrate on simplifying the network's perception of you while signalling the deeper talent that sits below the surface. The trick is simple complexity – selling you as a complex individual in a simple way.

Sell yourself

■ If you don't promote you, then who will?

■ 'Art is making something out of nothing and selling it.'

Frank Zappa

As you start to differentiate yourself in the network, you are selling yourself as a market product! Any good networker is trying to get other people to buy him/her as a person. When you sell yourself it is the combination of the four factors of symbolism, simplicity, singularity and sincerity that will enable your peers to remember who you are, what you do and how you can add value to them and their network.

The essence of good networking is in your ability to take these four factors and combine them into a single 60-second presentation. This 60-second pitch should allow you to present yourself to someone in the lift. Once the person buys this, then you may get the chance to do a five-minute pitch over coffee. This will lead to a 20-minute pitch in a meeting or the 60-minute pitch to use on a conference platform.

> When you sell yourself it is the combination of the four factors of symbolism, simplicity, singularity and sincerity that will enable your peers to remember who you are, what you do and how you can add value to them and their network.

■ **Simple**. Can you keep your personal pitch so simple that you could get the message across to someone in a crowded bar, over a couple of sips of beer? Look at any effective brand in the market and in most cases there is something memorable and very simple.

  – Can you describe you in a few words?
  – Could you describe you and what you do to a group of children so they understand?

Figure 7.3 4S pitch

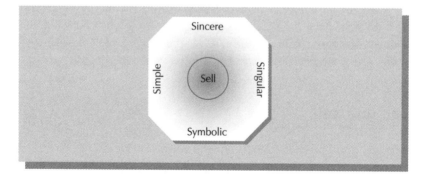

- **Singular**. You must appear to be unique in your network. Brand recognition needs to be instantaneous. The Red Cross symbol for medical care is unique and generally recognized across the world. Can you generate a simple and unique identity that your network will associate with you and no one else?

  – When you describe it does it remind you of anything?

  – If you tell a network peer what you do, what is the chance he/she will say 'oh that reminds me of . . . '?

- **Sincere**. People know when someone is faking it, so always ensure that your brand positioning description is true to your beliefs and values. If it is not authentic, you risk looking a bit stupid to those who really know you!

  – When your personal proposition is written down, does it feel comfortable to you?

  – When you describe it to others, is there some incredulity, or do they light up and say that it sounds just like you?

- **Symbolic**. It can really help to have a symbol that represents who you are and what you do.

  – When you describe your role, what feelings should it evoke in others?

  – Can you reframe it in the form of a parable or fairy story?

  – How would you draw it on the back of an envelope?

Imagine that you are sitting in a coffee bar and overhear one of your network members describing your personal proposition to another person: are you happy with the way he/she describes you? If not, then it suggests that you have failed to build and communicate your role in the network effectively.

In summary

Ask yourself:

- Have I really understood how I am unique and how to present this to the network?

- To what extent can I create a symbol that represents who I am and what I do?

- What does being authentic look like for me within the network?
- If I strip away the various things that I do, what is a simple statement that sums me up?
- Can I do a 60-second pitch to promote my value to a colleague?

'It always pays to assume a high trust until proved otherwise, rather than be too stingy at the start.'

Trevor Waldock

'Yes, you do have to work at it, and that is the hard part, but providing you have the trust going, it is easier to maintain. I know that there are people in the business that I haven't spoken to for ages, but because we have a shared understanding of our relationship, they can ask me for favours, and vice-versa, without expecting payback.'

Brenda Massey

Entrust others

Why *entrust* rather than *trust*?

- 'Work while you have the light. You are responsible for the talent that has been entrusted to you.'   *Henri F. Amiel*
- 'War is too serious a matter to entrust to military men.'
  Georges Clemenceau

The dictionary definition of entrust is: 'to give over (something) to another for care, protection, or performance'.[18] By virtue of joining a network I am explicitly and openly associating myself with other people. As such, I am entrusting my personal or professional brand to them. In the same way that the reputation of a restaurant will be closely linked to the quality of the food and wine it sells, so we can have our personal brand tarnished or enhanced by the behaviour of people in our network. I have to trust them and they have to trust me not to abuse this association.

Thus, the act of networking effectively asks us to entrust our personal capital to others. We are saying: 'here I am offering this gift of "me", please look after it in all your dealings with the market'.

Think about all the areas of your life where you entrust your brand to others:

- dropping your child off at playschool – *entrusting your child to the nurse*;
- yearly performance review – *entrusting your career to the boss*;
- eating from the local takeaway – *entrusting your health to the chef*;
- going on holiday – *entrusting the family to the airline pilot*;
- driving to work – *entrusting your life to other drivers*;
- paying for dinner – *entrusting your credit card to the waiter*.

Every day you are giving other people a part of you to do with as they wish. Every day you are giving a part of you to someone else who could seriously damage your family, health, finances or a host of other things. However, I am sure that where you are entrusting other people with important parts of your life there will be an internal flicker of suspicion. You will tacitly audit the person or situation by saying to yourself: 'is this OK – can I trust them not to damage me or my family?' The moment there is a suspicion of a rat in the local takeaway, the trust will be eroded and you will be less likely to entrust it with your health the next time you fancy a chicken kebab.

However, when it comes to brand, we happily entrust to other people one of our most valuable assets without really testing who they are and if we can really trust them. The whole notion of networking is built around a trust that binds people together and acts as a currency that flows around the network, much like the huge currency flows that circulate the globe in the blink of an eye.

Rights and responsibilities

Now, the notion of transferable trust brings with it quite significant responsibilities. If I entrust my child to someone, then I expect that person to take responsibility for my child's emotional and physical wellbeing, and if I put my car into the garage, I expect the garage to take responsibility for its upkeep.

Interestingly, we often entrust others with a right of control over our lives but don't quite believe they will be responsible in their use of the trust. When this happens we instinctively start to take precautions. We entrust the water company with our health but maybe boil the water before we drink it or use purification tablets; rather than trusting a national health service we might turn to private or alternative medicine; and if we have to trust what we know about the world to the press, then we will make sure that we read a spread of papers so as to seek out as close a representation of the truth as possible.[19]

This whole notion of entrusting others is intriguing, complex and potentially quite perilous. Just think about the number of times you entrust a part of you to others during the day. To what extent are you conscious of the process of entrusting others and are you clear as to the associated risks?

In the same way, when developing and maintaining your network you must be acutely conscious of the extent to which you are entrusting others: what you are entrusting them with; what responsibilities they accept with the entrustment; and finally what you expect in return for entrusting them with your brand. Only by being clear on this can you ensure that the trust currency which flows through the network will do so with ease and integrity.

In this section I aim to explore this idea further and introduce a trust framework that will help you to audit and assess the level of trust in your network and the extent to which you actually trust the various members of the community.

The key questions in this chapter are:

(a) What role does trust play in the formation and development of the network?

(b) What are the factors that impact on the choice of trust?

(c) How do I map and measure the levels of trust I have with other people?

(d) How do I use trust as a transferable commodity within the network?

(e) What are the deep reciprocal factors that drive how we entrust others?

How do I map and measure the levels of trust I have with other people?

Pressing the flesh and kissing babies

■ Trust is the oil that fuels the flow of social capital.

■ 'Love all, trust a few. Do wrong to none.'

William Shakespeare

Trust has a host of definitions. In a sales situation it can be a conviction or confidence in the honesty, integrity, and reliability of a product, service, brand or person. In a networking relationship the same criteria can apply, except that you are the product that people are using.

So how does trust link to networking or social capital? Francis Fukuyama suggests that social capital can be defined as an 'expectation that arises within a community of regular honest and corporative behaviour, based on commonly shared norms, on the part of other members in the community'.[20] So the more trust that is set up within a network, the greater level of cooperation and peer support that might be expected.

Thus, trust acts as an amplifier that can act upon itself. The more we give the more we get, which means we give more and so on. However, the reverse is also probably true and rapid attenuation can occur when mistrust sets in. This will rapidly turn the overall level of trust down within a network or community.

> The extent to which you can build trust is probably linked to the extent to which you can have social contact.

The extent to which you can build trust is probably linked to the extent to which you can have social contact. One finding of a number of surveys is that people are less inclined to trust institutions – like the medical profession 'in general' – but are more inclined to trust people they have contact with, like their doctor and especially the pharmacists. In surveys in the UK and the USA, pharmacists emerge as the people we trust the most.[21] The people we tend to trust most are those in our immediate circle of contact and experience. Interestingly, there is evidence that people are more willing to return to a company that has rectified a mistake than to one that has not made a mistake in the first place; the act of admitting the error confirms the authenticity of the relationship more than efficient delivery of a service.[22]

One might suspect that the only time we see politicians really hitting the streets is when an election is due. This might be because trust is a key part of the election process – because people are entrusting their state, security, street and safety to a stranger who will be making decisions about their life. But hold on – looking back at the previous statement – in general we don't trust institutions and we trust people who don't admit mistakes less – something that might be levelled at political institutions. I guess they are intuitively aware of this eroded trust which surfaces after the euphoria of each election victory (obviously only for one side) and thus the annual round of pressing the flesh and baby kissing as they try to rekindle the trust fund that has been seriously eroded over previous years.

> There is evidence that people are more willing to return to a company that has rectified a mistake than to one that has not made a mistake in the first place; the act of admitting the error confirms the authenticity of the relationship more than efficient delivery of a service.

One important point is that high-trust networks can be dangerous places to exist. Life would be wonderful if we could go around trusting everyone in anticipation that no one would ever let us down, steal things or copy our credit card number. The reality is that human beings are not always trustworthy and to believe otherwise would be foolish. These types of networks are vulnerable to parasites. In the land of the trustworthy the conman can become king.[23] In the same way that criminals will abuse those people who offer up a trust fund in credit, there are people around who will flagrantly abuse your network, even to the point of bringing it to an end because of the way they steal from the inbuilt trust funds. Because a network is a decentralized system without a single controller, it is very easy for someone to enter in the same way that a virus can invade a computer network and wipe out the system overnight.

Computer engineers develop anti-virus programs, companies use the selection process to filter out unwanted people, and society uses the legal system to identify and punish people. Maybe your network needs a system (formal or informal) that will help to identify and reject people who abuse the trust. My guess is that because the very nature of a network is a complex set of ties that will not be formally mapped, the management process will be informal.

> Because a network is a decentralized system without a single controller, it is very easy for someone to enter in the same way that a virus can invade a computer network and wipe out the system overnight.

It might be something as simple as the shunning process used by the Amish in Pennsylvania. They have a process whereby they ignore or do not respond to those people who break their social code or cause problems in the community. They shun them and turn them into non-persons.

The trust choice

- In the blink of an idea we can give away our prized asset – our personal brand.
- 'Those who trust to chance must abide by the results of chance.'
  Calvin Coolidge

Imagine yourself as you walk into a training centre as you are faced with 30 people with whom you are about to spend a two-day training course. Over the two days you will form a variety of opinions on these people. One of the strongest views that will be formed is to what extent you trust each of them. As you leave the event you will have made either an explicit or implicit choice about the extent to which you trust each of the delegates. This choice will have a direct and consequential impact upon which of these people ultimately join your network.

The actual process of trusting someone can be quite complex. Four factors that will have an impact are the level of awareness or consciousness of the process (explicit or tacit) and the source of the choice (head or heart). These can be described as follows:

- **Explicit trust**. Sometimes trust takes a very overt form. For instance, most of us trust that the authorized driver teaching our child or partner to drive has been screened, tested and qualified to manage the car in dangerous or difficult situations. These explicit credentials can be seen in their certified qualifications. Or, we explicitly trust that our independent financial adviser will find the best place to invest our money based upon his/her qualifications.

■ **Tacit trust**. Trust also takes an implicit form. For instance, every time we open a tin of beans, we trust that it will taste as expected. Or, when we ask a friend for some advice we implicitly trust that our friend will be honest with us. In these cases, trust is an unconscious benchmark from which the customer judges the quality of service. In other words, there is no conscious or overt process to test or assure the standards of the product until the product lets us down.

■ **Head trust**. This is the cognitive type of trust where we pause to think for a second 'do I trust the person or product that I am dealing with?'. This might be that second you take to look over the motorbike that you have just hired from the back street hire shop on holiday. Or it might be to count the change in a shop where you were short-changed in the past.

■ **Heart trust**. This is the emotional or gut feel assessment that we take to form an opinion. There are some people we just emotionally buy into and accept that they are OK to work with, whereas with others it just doesn't feel right (even if they have all the right certificates and qualifications).

If we bring these four types of trust together we have the basic trust frame-work shown in Figure 8.1. This indicates the four different ways that we use trust to develop and maintain our network.

Figure 8.1　The four types of trust

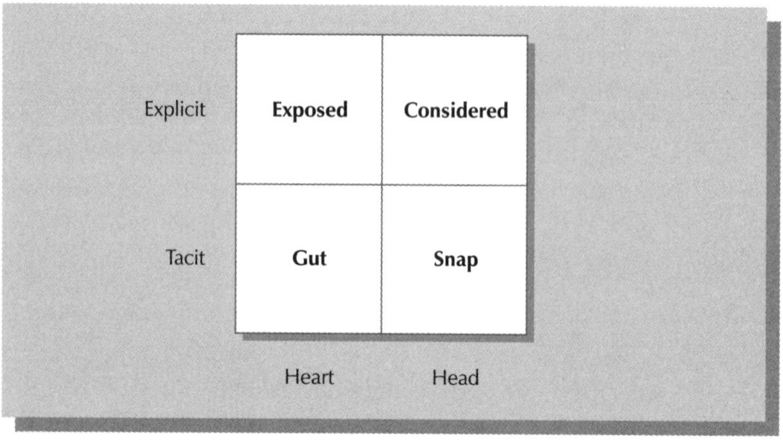

- **Gut**. The gut is a sudden yes/no choice that happens when you meet someone. Sometimes you don't even know that you have made the choice to trust someone as it happens so fast. It is the real emotional buy-in to someone without knowing why. The benefit is that it just happens for you and in many cases the person will intuitively understand that you have bought into him and so the level of trust can be reciprocated. The down side is pretty obvious, that is, it is the wrong decision. I know of one person who swore by his gut decisions when he recruited people. The trouble was that most of the time he ended up in abysmal failure – but he still carried on believing!

- **Snap**. This is very similar to the gut choice, but this time it comes from the cognitive elements rather than emotional ones. As such, the choice will come from lessons learned in the past that have helped to form the assumptions and mental maps that are used to make sense of the world. These are often known as heuristic or rules of thumb choices. So in your experience you might have found that people who have worked for a certain company can be trusted. This might not always be true, but at an intuitive level and based on previous experience you then tend to use it as a rule of thumb.

- **Considered**. This trust choice is made both overtly and cognitively. For this one you might sit down and really think about someone and decide if you want to trust him or her. After meeting someone you might decide to reserve judgment, talk to other people about the person, sit down, mull it over, weigh up the pros and cons before coming to your final decision. The plus is that this should be a robust choice, but the down side is a risk of paralysis from analysis. You might take so long to signal your view that the person might decide not to trust you.

- **Exposed**. This process is quite an interesting one because it is being consciously managed but by tapping into the emotional elements. This is a process where you might sit down and ask yourself how you really feel about this person. What does my heart tell me about this relationship and how will it feel to be in a network partnership with this person? The benefit is one of taking enough time to really test the heart and see if it feels OK. The down side might be that it could appear somewhat cold to the other person, especially if you explain how you are making the choice about working with him or her. The other difficulty is that the whole process of making explicit what are often tacit emotions can be challenging, especially if you are used to working in a work environment that is very formal or logical – the type of place where soft stuff is only for pussycats.

There are two key points regarding the framework. First, trust is the primary currency that underpins and holds a network together and helps it to function. With most professional networks there is no hierarchy, rules of office or governance systems, they just happen because people want the community to exist. The second point is that since trust is the primary currency, we must be very careful of the way in which it is traded. We make choices every day or maybe every hour about whom to entrust ourselves or our brand. We must make this choice carefully and be aware of the consequences of investing in the wrong person and the gain that can be achieved by investing in the right person.

To do this it helps to be more conscious of your trust choices. Do you have a tendency to go for a gut decision? Are you more cautious and think things through, or do you tend to make snap decisions that seem right? There is no right choice but the important thing is to be conscious of your preferences. Once understood, it becomes easier to step between the four quadrants and make a trust choice based upon the person and the context rather than doing what you normally do.

One final step might be to become more conscious of the processes that others use to make trust choices about you. If you meet someone who seems to go for a gut reaction about you in the first 10 seconds, is that because you are such a trustworthy and wonderful person, or does the person do that with everyone he/she meets? Ask yourself if you are confident about people's trust-choice process. This is important because if you go into a network with them, you will be entrusting your brand to their control, and are you confident that they will not erode it because they fall into trust too easily with other people, people with whom you would sooner not associate your personal brand?

Trust funds

■ The accumulation of a trust fund takes time and effort and cannot be achieved though easy pickings.

Trust is the fulcrum that can affect different degrees of leverage in a network. By shifting the fulcrum in the high-trust direction, you can quantify the reduction in time taken to solve problems and work effectively. Correspondingly, as the fulcrum shifts the other way, trust diminishes, power battles erupt, tribal camps form and the flows of value and abundance are weakened.

However, trust isn't a simple switch that can be turned on and off at will. The giving and taking of trust can vary considerably in its fragility and resilience, and can change quickly or slowly depending on the circumstances. Trust associated with a close personal friendship is resilient and durable, and might be regarded as *thick trust*. Once established, it's not easily disrupted, but once shattered, it is not readily repaired or restored. Alternatively, in casual or short-term relationships, we might see *thin trust*. This is the type conferred on a project group or product team, where people tend to commit only part of themselves.

The problem with trust is that it's like a good partnership – you know it when you see it, but it's hard to define the individual contributory factors. As an example, think about someone you know well and trust implicitly. What is it that makes you think of that person? What do you both do to maintain the relationship? Now think of another person you know just as well but don't trust. Consider what it is that each of you does to create a relationship lacking in substance and value. What's the impact of such a relationship and what overheads does it impose? If you ask the person to do a job or help you out, to what extent do you have to give up valuable personal time to check and oversee the work? Do you lose sleep because there is a fear in the back of your mind that he/she might not deliver on time?

The time you spend building your network is an investment process, where you choose to offer and invest your personal resources and capital to create social capital for future payback. If you end up spending a large chunk of your time with people who turn out to be untrustworthy, it feels awful. To what extent do you have network partners where this exists? To what extent would you pay your wages into an account that offers a reduced return? In the same way, it is important to ensure that you don't invest your personal capital in a social capital fund that will not repay a compound return.

Network relationships are like savings accounts – we put time and energy into them in the hope that the social capital will grow and multiply, in the same way that investments in a financial fund will produce compound growth over time. It may appear artificial and false to measure the level of your social capital with your network connections, but like your finances, you should be aware of the amounts that you've invested in different places; monitor the levels of abundance with each person, and where necessary, make changes to improve the return.

Managing your investment

There is a simple definition of trust that can be used to measure and manage the nature of a relationship:

- **T**ruthful – the extent to which integrity, honesty and truthfulness are developed and maintained.
- **R**esponsive – the openness, mental accessibility or willingness to share ideas and information freely.

- **U**niform – the degree of consistency, reliability and predictability contained within the relationship.

- **S**afe – the loyalty, benevolence or willingness to protect, support and encourage each other.

- **T**rained – the competence, technical knowledge and capabilities of both parties.

Where these five attributes are soundly in place, the nature of the relationship might have the characteristics of a thick trust interaction. Conversely, where one or more of the factors is diminished or missing, it's possible that the relationship is suffering from thin trust.

To what extent do you manage the trust levels with people you work with and care for? In the same way that you have credits and debits with your bank, you also have a trust fund with all the people you interact with where debits and credits are applied on a daily basis.

As I look at my current network, there are people where the trust fund is really in joint credit and supports a synergistic relationship. We both invest heavily in the network tie and reap terrific benefits. There is another person where I have been draining the fund lately because I have been getting more than giving and have not really been responsive to the person's needs. This relationship is very much at a selfish level from my perspective. Or, there is another where I introduced the person to a client and then the person tried to sell to the client behind my back. As a consequence, I don't feel safe giving such a person access to any other part of my client network. In this case the individual is in debit with me and needs to do a lot of work to get back into credit.

For any relationship it's very easy for us to move the account sliders on the account into credit or debit, as seen in Figure 8.2. When working with

Figure 8.2   Trust fund

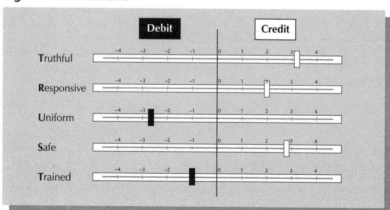

a client I have only to falsify a client reference to weaken the 'Truthful' slider; ignore some of the client's requests for help for him/her to feel that I'm not being 'Responsive'; tell the client different things at different times to upset the 'Uniform' balance; be indiscreet about someone else to raise concerns about how safe the client feels telling me personal issues; or appear not to be competent in my diagnoses to reduce the value in the 'Trained' sub-account. Slippage in any one area of the trust fund erodes the value of my personal capital and, even worse, reduces my chance to create a shared success with the person at a later date.

Making deposits and withdrawing credits on your trust fund is not as easy as you might think. Just do someone a favour and you're in credit, or upset him or her and you're in debit. But life isn't quite that simple. Imagine the boss at work who organized a thank-you event for the team. He wants to repay everyone for all the hard work over the year. So he arranges a surprise visit to a theme park, dinner in the evening and then an overnight stop at a plush hotel. All goes well and he leaves the team the next day believing that everyone will feel rewarded and, as a result, that he has made some great deposits in the trust fund. What he doesn't realize is that two people in the team are scared of heights and had a terrible experience when they were persuaded to go on the high rides by other team members; another three were vegetarian and the restaurant's only vegetarian dish was crab salad; finally, four members of the team didn't really want to be away from their family and just really wanted to go home. The net result was that the trust fund was diminished (on a number of levels) for many people and they would not want to go on another team event organized by him.

> The challenge is to think about the credit/debit relationship, and if you really want to make a deposit in someone's trust fund, make sure you understand that individual's map; don't impose your own.

Think about how you currently work with people in your network. To what extent are you giving them credits that might be perceived as debits? Do you take people out for a beer to celebrate, even if they want a coffee? Do you share confidences with other people in the network? Do you understand what they want from you? The challenge is to think about the credit/debit relationship, and if you really want to make a deposit in someone's trust fund, make sure you understand that individual's map; don't impose your own.

Trust-fund networks

If this seems foreboding, think about how many people are in your network. For each person you'll have a separate and unique trust fund that is either in debit or credit. The list is endless and probably growing every day.

Figure 8.3 shows a network of four people in a community. For each of them I might aspire to maintain a relationship that is always in credit, but often fail to do so. The problem occurs when conflict develops between the needs of the different players in my world. While it's important for me to spend professional time with A and B to develop a thick-trust relationship, it means that I give up time with C and D. This inner conflict can lead to a real problem in trying to maintain effective relationships, and also lead to increased personal turmoil.

Figure 8.3 Trust Fund Networks

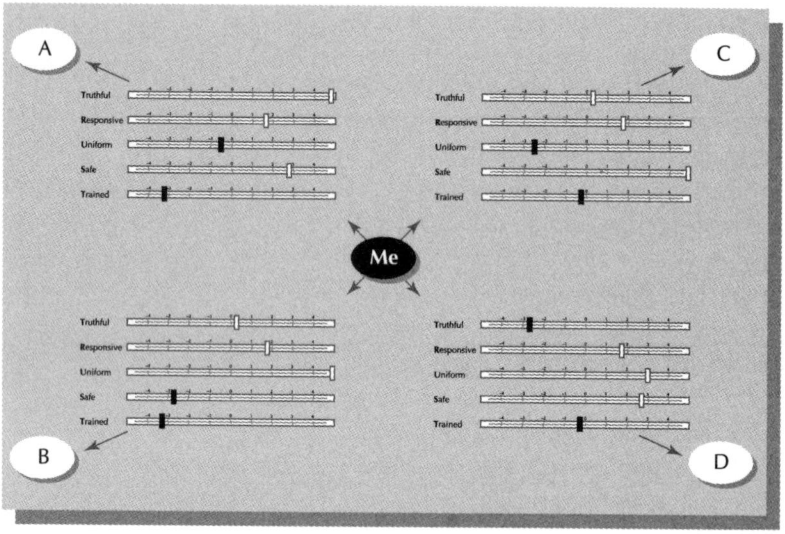

It's relatively easy to establish trust in small communities where everyone knows your name. Where people are on a first-name basis, trust can be open and manageable. The difficulty arises in establishing trust funds when the community grows to a size where not everyone knows or remembers your name. The exact size at which this happens will depend on the type and form of your network, but growing pains often begin at the point at which anyone in the network no longer expects to interact with others on a regular basis. When the transaction shifts from natural top-up to forced encounter, there is a real danger of trust-fund failure.

When this happens we immediately hit two problems: authentication and authorization. First, people no longer know who the other people are and how they came into the self-managed network. This is the authentication problem. Second, you become wary of who is gaining entry to other people in your network. Who is 'slingshooting' through your network to get access to someone you value and care for? This is the authorization problem.

These factors really touch only the surface issues that underpin the formation of a network. Although some might feel that this is overkill, with too much effort being applied on a minor factor, my belief is that it is important to be conscious of the trust funds that flow round the network and, as a consequence, the extent to which you are prepared to entrust your brand to others. If you don't make these decisions consciously, then how are you making them? Maybe gut decisions can be effective, but often the heart-ruled choice can lead to disastrous trust choices which can in turn have a serious impact on your value and role within the network.

> The difficulty arises in establishing trust funds when the community grows to a size where not everyone knows or remembers your name.

The nature of any trust fund will never stay static. It will shift and vary over time as people make debits and credits. It is important to understand the nature of this journey, the patterns it will take and what you can do to speed up the changes in the journey without destroying the underlying value of the social capital.

Transferable trust

One of the things I find most challenging and irritating is trying to find a good tradesman, someone who can do things around the house that I am rubbish at. So many times I have had someone come round to do some work and all we end up with is a repair that looks fine initially, but after a while problems start to surface. I am always left with a complete sense of frustration: just how on earth can I find someone who will do a job for me, someone I can trust and who will not rip me off in the process?

My solution has recently been to talk to Mike and Dave, who run our local hardware store. Instead of searching the local yellow pages I just ask them whom they would recommend. The difference has been amazing: everyone that we have used on their recommendation has been clean, efficient, effective and absolutely trustworthy.

Now, this is a very simple example of trust management but is fundamental to the whole process of managing an effective network. The first thing to note is that I trust Mike and Dave enough to value their judgment. This is a trust fund that has been building over many years of buying from their store. Taking this relationship against the trust fund index:

- Truthful. They have never lied to me about a product I have bought. If I have a problem, they will tell me if they have a solution. If not, they will point me to somewhere else that can help me.

- Responsive. So often I go in to see them without buying anything – just to pick their brains – and they have never turned me away or said they are too busy.

- Uniform. No matter which of the two brothers I talk to, the response will be the same.

- Safe. I believe that anything I tell them stays with them and doesn't get fed to the rumour or gossip machine in the neighbourhood. A large part of this comfort comes from the fact that I don't hear them bad mouth other people behind their backs, so there is some evidence that they are not talking about me behind my back (hopefully).

- Trained. They always seem to know the answer or know someone who does.

For me the trust fund is well into credit so I am happy to turn to them for advice. Interestingly, looking at some of the research mentioned before, I am less inclined to trust the big 'branded' DIY stores, because they seem to continually get into debit on the trust fund with me, particularly around the 'Trained' area. Much of this is because of the tendency to employ very young people who just don't have the years of wisdom that Mike and Dave have.

A number of local builders use the store and over a period of time they get to know these people and more importantly their reputation. Much of this will come from word of mouth within that specialized community. They form an opinion as to who the good builders are and what it is they do well. My gain comes from the ability to tap into the trust fund by exploiting whom they trust for my benefit. The result of this is they were happy to recommend a builder called Nick to help me out.

The great thing about the trust fund is that it is like a wrapper that sits around the person, in the same way as when you open a box of sweets, undo the wrapper and put the sweet in your mouth. The wrapper offers you some comfort that the sweet has been packed to a quality level and thus it is something that you don't need to worry about. So by asking Mike and

Figure 8.4 An example of trust management

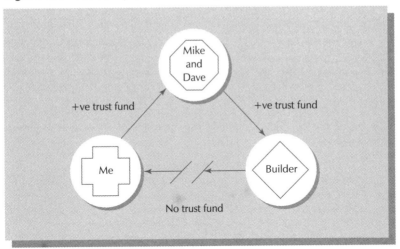

Dave who they would recommend, they are passing on a builder who comes ready enfolded in a trust wrapper. This means that all I have to do is accept the trust in Nick the builder, as transferred by the shop and assume it as a given.

The ability to use this currency of transferable trust offers quite significant benefits. For me it probably saved two days of grief. Just imagine having to get three or four builders to come to look at the job, give a price, check references and finally find someone I could work with. Effectively this is two days of trying to grow the trust fund with someone to a point where I am happy for the person to do the work and wander unsupervised around the house. The transferable trust from Mike and Dave saved all of this in one hit. This gives a simple example of the 'weak tie' connection mentioned in Chapter 6. By having a weak link with the guys at the shop, I could exploit this value and make huge time and cost savings.

> By building up intra-trust funds across the network, the efficiencies can be quite huge as people build references and pass 'wrapped' people onto other people where they know their services can be of benefit to all players in the relationship.

Now relate this to your professional network. By building up intra-trust funds across the network, the efficiencies can be quite huge as people build references and pass 'wrapped' people onto other people where they know their services can be of benefit to all players in the relationship.

An important thing about transferable trust concerns the word 'entrust'. By linking me with Nick the builder, Mike and Dave are taking a gamble. If the builder lets me down, then a debit is applied to their trust fund with me. Now this might not be fair but it is life. If you recommend someone as valuable within a network, you are wrapping your brand around theirs and will probably have to suffer the consequences, for little or no reward. However, the reverse is also true, if I were to be a bad customer to the builder, then it might be the last time he takes a recommendation from them.

By giving me the builder's details, they are entrusting me with their business brand for a short period. I have to accept the rights that I get from having access to them as a network connection but also be aware of the responsibility this confers on me to not erode their brand value.

> To trust something or someone is to honour an institution or individual with your good regard. To enjoy the trust of others is to enjoy a compliment to your reputation.

Trust means a lot. To trust something or someone is to honour an institution or individual with your good regard. To enjoy the trust of others is to enjoy a compliment to your reputation. Trust is vital to network cohesion and is a quality that never diminishes in importance. For a networker, trust is essential to everything we do. Trust's principles are fundamental to the wellbeing of a relationship between you and your network and with the external clients of the network. People need to trust brands. Brands need that trust. In short: *brand equals trust*.

Give to get – reciprocity

■ 'To the extent to which one makes happiness the objective of his motivation, he necessarily makes it the object of his attention. But precisely by so doing he loses sight of the reason for happiness, and happiness itself must fade away.'

Viktor E. Frankl, The Will to Meaning

■ 'All men are caught in an inescapable network of mutuality.'

Martin Luther King Jr.

The key element about 'entrusting others' is that you are giving something to someone. Something that is often quite intangible but very valuable for both you and the recipient. At this stage then a gift is changing hands as a transaction in the same way that a child will give you a kiss, a husband might buy his wife some flowers or you will spot a book that you believe someone will like and buy it for him/her as a surprise present.

The rule of reciprocity

But . . . when you buy that gift for someone, are you doing it for that person or are you doing it for you? Have you bought the present as a single one-way transaction with no thought about getting a present in return; or deep down might you hope that the recipient will reciprocate at some later stage (maybe by getting you a book or doing a favour of value to you)?

Although the 'entrust others' stage can seem fluffy and woolly, it is actually a highly audited process of reciprocity where we measure the extent to which our giving of the gift of trust to others is reciprocated. Although this may seem clinical, it is a process of self-protection that ensures we don't erode the value of our personal brand and social capital.

Reciprocity simply means that if you do something for a colleague (such as referring him to a client), the colleague might be compelled to do something for you in return.[24] This is a natural human action that will happen in any society where all members of the culture learn from a young age to abide by the (spoken and unspoken) rule or suffer serious social disapproval. This sense of future indebtedness makes possible the development of various kinds of continuing relationships, transactions, and exchanges that are fundamental to society's wellbeing and the overall rule of law and governance.

> This sense of future indebtedness makes possible the development of various kinds of continuing relationships, transactions, and exchanges that are fundamental to society's wellbeing and the overall rule of law and governance.

While Westerners often think of 'primitive' or non-market economies as static 'subsistence systems' (i.e., geared only to the limited needs of local populations), in fact they can operate around sophisticated trading relationships. In Papua New Guinea, status is earned by giving things away rather than acquiring them. This is known as the Moka, a ceremony in which people, sometimes whole tribes, give gifts to members of other tribes. The larger the gift, the greater the victory of the recipient. The trick with the Moka exchange is the obligation to return an equal amount plus more. It is a system of incremental exchange, not of balanced trade. People are locked into escalating relations of generosity and debt. This is why wealth is a sign of personal prowess, and more a measure of what you give than what you receive.[25]

I got caught by this last Christmas during a family holiday in Spain. We all decided to go out for a meal to a local restaurant. Now the meal was OK but nothing special. The service was reasonable and the food was quite edible. At the end of the evening I asked for the bill and just as I had finished paying and we were about to walk out one of the staff gave my wife a small Christmas present. Now in reality it was a simple toy that made a few silly noises. However, we were thrilled with the fact that we had been given a gift. So the following night we were out walking and looking for somewhere to eat; as we walked along the front we went past the same restaurant and the manager smiled at us. Immediately, almost without thinking we walked back into the restaurant for another meal. Now with the benefit of hindsight I realized that the revisit was nothing to do with the quality of the food, it was just that they had given us a gift and we wanted to reciprocate the kindness.

Sitting underneath the idea of reciprocity are a number common factors:

- **Feel the force**. The need to pay back a gift or something that has been entrusted to you is a very powerful emotional and social force. It is so strong that we often feel compelled to pay people back a favour even if we don't like them or they have done something to offend us in giving the gift.

- **First-mover control**. Even when someone initiates a favour that we don't want, we are automatically placed into a debt position. This gives amazing power to other people to effect control over what we think, feel and do, almost without our realizing it.

- **Arms race**. To be rid of the uncomfortable feeling of indebtedness, people will sometimes agree to a request for a substantially larger favour than the one he or she first received. If the original giver then reciprocates, a race can begin to out-reciprocate the other person. We are then into a potential increasing race to outdo the other person.

- **Pure abundance**. Where people are able to give without any expectation of a gift back, then we are moving towards a pure level of altruistic abundance. One that people may aspire to or say that they do but which can be very difficult to maintain when little or nothing is reciprocated.

- **Blind faith**. Any act of abundance will build your fund of social capital. This will hopefully create a network of embedded potential reciprocity. The important thing is that those you do the favour for may not be those who return it. The help you give may be return from a ripple effect where two, three or four degrees of separation may sit between your donation and the final receipt. The only way that abundant reciprocity can work is if you have belief in the idea rather than the measured return or payback on the investment. This might be similar to the idea of shelter huts in the wild that are maintained for a collective purpose, where all will use the asset but ensure they leave it well stocked for the next person.

- **Faking it**. There is one really common process that is driven more by self-interest than any interest for abundant reciprocity. This is called the 'rejection-then-retreat' technique. This is based on the idea that you offer someone an extreme request that you know the person will never agree to; once rejected, you can offer to reduce your request. By the process of reducing your initial request you have planted a favour seed of a concession. The duplicitous factor is that this is probably the one the person wanted in the first place.

- **Sweat the small stuff**. Think about the last time you were given a business card and didn't have one to return. The internal tension can be quite awful, and this tension may well include a big chunk of guilt about looking unprofessional. The lesson is that often it is the little things can create the most impact in the reciprocity game.

- **Beware the big gift**. You must also beware the problem of giving someone too much trust in the wrong context. You can give someone a huge present and the recipient might think you are (a) up to no good, (b) full of spare cash, (c) after something. Reciprocity can backfire when it appears too aggressive and over the top.

It is rare that a gift will be offered in isolation. There may well be some form of interest behind the donation or receipt. As a consequence, there are at least three donation or giver types and three potential reciprocal or receiver types.

Giver types

(a) The gift might be given in pure abundance, i.e. with no expectation of any payback (*give to give*).

(b) There might be intent to view it as an investment in the relationship with anticipation of a favour returned at some point in the future (*give to invest*).

(c) The giver might make the payment and expect to receive payback immediately (*give to get*).

Receiver types

(a) The recipient might accept it in isolation as a unitary gift, and so the transaction is closed and no reciprocity will be offered (*get*).

(b) The recipient might move into a soft reciprocal mode and believe that he/she will return the favour one day (*get and invest*).

(c) The receiver might feel subordinate to the other person and consequently need to return a gift to close the feeling of debt (*get then give*).

These six patterns can be seen in Figure 8.5. This framework shows six different types of reciprocal actions that can be involved in a 1:1 engagement.

However, if you think about people who you have transacted with over the past week, then you might see that you have given one type of donation in anticipation of receiving a reciprocal response but maybe received an unexpected reply. For example, one of your connections has been looking for a job and you noticed a post in the local paper that would be ideal for her. You decided to send the paper over and suggest that she follow up on the job. For you this is a 'give' transaction. There is little cost to you in making the donation and you made the gesture from a pure abundance point of view with no anticipation of a favour being offered in return. However, the moment the paper is received, she contacts you to say thanks and suggests that she take you out for dinner as a reward for helping her out. Now, if your donation was a 'give to get' transaction, the response might be appropriate, but as it was a simple 'give', the effusive response can almost feel awkward. It was a gift and you have no requirement for a payback. If anything, the fact that she feels the need to return the favour makes you wonder about the nature of the relationship.

The converse can be true where someone helps a friend out with a 'give to invest' donation and then waits, and waits, and waits for the response

Figure 8.5 Reciprocity map

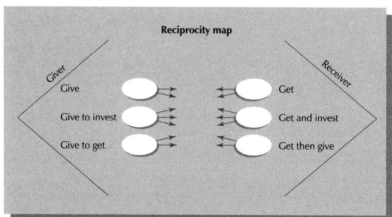

but nothing is forthcoming. The giver decides that the other person does not value the friendship and so decides to close down the connection. The trouble is that the receiver believed it was a simple 'give' donation and did not see any reason to return the favour. As a consequence, the connection starts to drift and decay with neither side really understanding why the shadow has been cast across the relationship.

What should be seen from these two examples is that where the giver and receiver types are in congruence, the reciprocity process will be in balance. However, where the types are unwittingly varied, real relational problems can emerge, often without either side understanding why.

The complexity of this can be seen if we look at the relationship between the six reciprocity types and the nine transactional states that can emerge when they are enacted (Table 8.1).

At the end of the day it helps to understand how reciprocity works and the impact it has on our personal lives. The positive aspect is that the embedded sense of future obligation and personal debt makes possible the development of various kinds of relationships, transactions and exchanges that are so beneficial to society. This includes political, legal and even the bartering process that underpins the complex relationships when countries avoid a war. However, it can also be a destructive process that leads to conflict in the school playground, conflict in the commercial world and tension between nation states as they play games.

As you start to grow and maintain your network, the notion of reciprocity is something that you need to be very conscious of, especially as you begin entrusting people with your personal brand. Questions to be considered include: who do you entrust your brand with? Why are you entrusting them? How will the receiver view the gift? What reciprocal action will the receiver take and how will you respond to his/her action? The act of giving can actively grow your social capital, but beware, there might be a down side and it is important to make sure that you are not getting into Moka relationships, where the focus is on the giving and getting rather than deriving mutual benefit from the network association.

Table 8.1 Reciprocity types and transactional states

Giver	Receiver	Impact
1. **Give**	**Get**	Balanced transaction that leaves both players happy
2. **Give**	**Get and invest**	Reasonably balanced, although the giver might be confused if the receiver responds at a later date
3. **Give**	**Get, then give**	Out of balance, may confuse the giver when the transaction is reciprocated so rapidly
4. **Give to invest**	**Get**	Initially in balance but the giver may get confused later if he/she does not feel that the transaction is reciprocated
5. **Give to invest**	**Get and invest**	Balanced transaction where the social capital should grow over time
6. **Give to invest**	**Get, then give**	May confuse the giver because he/she is expecting a long-term investment and all of a sudden gets an unexpected payback
7. **Give to get**	**Get**	Will confuse both the giver and receiver. The giver will be looking for a rapid payback but if the receiver doesn't know this it may lead to shadow problems
8. **Give to get**	**Get and invest**	Again, the receiver will accept it as tradable process but not look for instant reciprocation
9. **Give to get**	**Get, then give**	In balance because both players see this as instant response. The one risk is that they get into a bidding war and it escalates out of balance

In summary

Ask yourself:

- To what extent do I entrust my brand to others in the network and to what extent do others entrust me with theirs?
- What preferences do I have in the way that trust is formed – do I need to learn to shift to a different type of trust formation?
- What is the level of my trust fund with each of the key networks nodes?
- Do I transfer my trust fund to others without realizing it and what impact does this have on my brand value within the network?
- What is my reciprocal preference – do I give, give to invest or give to get?

'You have to keep relationships alive – you need to meet, ring, eat and drink together. To create relationships in the networks you have to prepare the soil, till it, plant the seeds, nurture them, develop them, allow them to grow and then finally reap the harvest. For me this is relationship management as farming rather than scavenging and hunting.'

Anton Fishman

'The good networkers for me are not cut-throat users. The ones who build a sustainable network are those who recognize the "I know a man who can" value of relationships. Knowing that longer term works just like a good investment put away for capital growth rather than short-term gain.'

Kenny Whitson

Fuel the flow

Although we might talk about 'the network', it doesn't actually exist. It is not a unitary or solid asset; it is simply a contrived act between groups of people who come together for mutual benefit. To view the network as a separate asset would essentially give it a life and suggest that it can operate as a closed system or separate unit. In reality the network is an open system. It is always part of a wider environment and cannot be dissociated from the world in which it sits for a personal convenience.

As an open system it survives because of the interaction with its surrounding world. External stimuli can come from meeting new people, generating audacious ideas, identifying new market opportunities. This is often the easy and fun part in setting up the network. The really hard part comes in trying to hold it together. The ongoing management needed to maintain this continuous source of external stimuli can be quite draining.

In the same way that you might take time at the end of each week to keep a check on the house or office finances, check the car oil or make sure that you have thrown out the mouldy cheese and milk from the fridge, you need to check and update your social system. This can feel like tax on your time. You might be all set to go to the café with some friends, play pool down at the club or hit the mall for some serious shopping but suddenly you realize that there are people you promised to contact but failed to send the e-mails. What do you do? The heart says shop, shop, shop, while the head drags you back to reality and says (like the yearly tax return) invest 30 minutes now and you will save a week at the back end of the year.

As your network expands and becomes ever more complex, you will need a certain set of management routines that will ensure that the flow of social capital is not stymied by relationship problems. Hence, when we talk about network management in the social capital context we might define it as a process of controlling your social network so as to optimize its efficiency and productivity.

There is a real danger in this section that much of what I am going to consider will provoke a negative response. This is because I am suggesting that we might have to raise to the surface many of the shadow or undiscussible factors used to manage a social network but rarely discussed openly. As a consequence, some people might feel that the approaches offered are manipulative, political and outright Machiavellian. Whilst I would support the feelings, I would ague that the logic is flawed. If these are things that we do in the shadow, then surfacing the issues and making them discussible must aid effective network management and the creation of sustainable social capital. If people are using their network for personal gain, power or exploitation, so the process will become visible and people can start to challenge any duplicitous behaviour driving the networking model. So bear with me and read through to the end. If you do feel that the ideas will stimulate a manipulative approach, then by all means drop me a note and we can have a dialogue about the nature of surface versus shadow networking.

The five areas considered in this section are:

1. the natural dynamics of a network growth and decay cycle;
2. the common problems which can cause a network to flounder;
3. the need to manage memes to prevent network corruption;
4. how network structure differs from a formal organization;
5. the process of knowledge diffusion and the role in network-flow processes.

Riding the network S-curve

- The process of decay starts the moment a work of art is complete.
- The role of the curator is to prolong the life of something and defer the inevitable.

OK – so the network is set up, you are buzzing, interactive with all these people and things are looking great – that is for about a month. Then you find that some people aren't returning your calls, others want to meet you on the same day at the same time. Over the period of a month it is very easy for a network to go from a vibrant collection of people who want to interact to a group who are disenfranchised and looking elsewhere for support.

There is a natural entropic tendency that pulls the community back to its normal state, i.e. a collection of separate individuals rather than a community centred on a belief or set of values. This is why organizations need rules, procedures and governance processes to stop the process of decay and keep the organization together in a unitary form. Professional networks don't have this and the end result is like herding cats – pretty impossible; without some network management process to help fuel the flow of abundance through the network, it may well collapse.

This rapid rise and decay can be seen in the classical S-curve that drives all societal and technological change (Figure 9.1). Technological development typically follows an 'S' pattern. For example, technologies will often take 20 years to become an overnight success. They start at point (a) as an emerging idea, start to grow once the market becomes aware, 20 years later it takes off, suddenly rising vertically hitting point (b).

> You find that some people aren't returning your calls, others want to meet you on the same day at the same time. Over the period of a month it is very easy for a network to go from a vibrant collection of people who want to interact to a group who are disenfranchised and looking elsewhere for support.

Then the top 'cap' of the 'S' takes over with a straight line, and the letter is complete. In terms of the Internet, we are in all probability still at point (a) and the real shift in performance will come in a few years' time once market maturity kicks in.

The more decentralized a system, the more it takes on aspects of organic growth. Growing things share several universal characteristics. The key fea-

Figure 9.1 S-curve

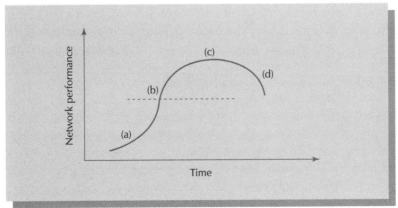

ture is the S-shaped curve: slow birth, steep growth and slow decline. The worldwide production of cars per year or the lifetime production of symphonies composed by Mozart both fit an S-curve with great precision. What the graceful shape of the S-curve offers is the fact that natural growth obeys a strict law: the shape of the ending is symmetrical to the shape of the beginning. The law is based on empirical observations of thousands of biological and institutional life histories. The law is closely related to the natural distribution of complex things as expressed in a bell curve. Although early growth can be susceptible to the initial conditions that are faced when emerging, once on a roll, the shape can be fairly predictable.

> Growing things share several universal characteristics. The key feature is the S-shaped curve: slow birth, steep growth and slow decline.

Not every network growth will show a smooth S-curve lifespan, but a remarkable number are likely to. Our job as a member of the community is to understand that this trajectory is a natural phenomenon and do all that we can to lengthen the time duration and so defer the final demise of the network until a point that the death is timely and suitable for all members.

The dynamics of a network 'S'-curve are as follows. In the beginning (a), expansion is slow because the people are adapting to each other and the environment in which they are operating. When the relationships in the community mature, the growth becomes fast (b). The very pace of growth leads the community into a new world, which has new operating principles, goals and distributed leadership. Although the factors aid the growth process in the early days, they can offer problems once the system gets to maturity. The skills and knowledge that led to the growth (b) are now inappropriate for continued growth (success) (c). But the community may find it hard to let go of the old ways of thinking which help to create the initial success (b). Like the successful animal that adapts and changes according to the changes in the environment, the network may have to give up some of its old ways of thinking, feeling and behaving in order to succeed and develop further. Failure to do so leads to decline (d).

Very often the way performance is maintained and enhanced is by not rebuilding the current activities, but by reframing the situation and creating a new S-curve to take the network operation to a higher level, in the same way that a car company will update a range of cars for a while to maintain market currency and performance. However, at some point it will go for a redesign and release a totally new concept.

Building the network can be quite easy, the hard work comes in trying to maintain the community once it is up and running. This is because all human communities will ebb and flow, like a tide washing back and forth on a beach. The trick is to step back from the periodic ebbs and be conscious of the overall performance trend of the network as seen in Figure 9.3.

So far we have considered 'the network' performance curve. But the problem is that the network is simply a collection of

While the goal of 'fuel the flow' is to ensure that the network follows a series of repeating S-curves, the actual intervention and management will be by managing people's individual S-curves.

Figure 9.2 The network S-curve

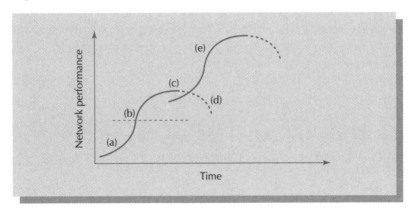

Figure 9.3 Network performance flow

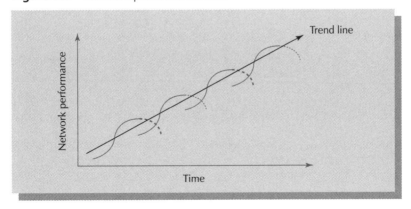

disparate people who each have their own journey as individuals and as part of the network. While the goal of 'fuel the flow' is to ensure that the network follows a series of repeating S-curves, the actual intervention and management will be by managing people's individual S-curves.

You must choose what interventions you should make with people to help them progress up the network. To do this you must determine a number of points. Where are they on their own S-curve? Do they really want to be part of your network? How many other networks are they part of and is this too many? Do you want them to go up the S-curve or should you shut the relationship down? The factors to consider are endless, but the key thing is to not take the individual in isolation when you are looking at his or her performance within the network. Look at their trend and understand that (like you) the person will be on a developmental cycle. Sometimes your connections might be happy and enthusiastic to meet up for coffee and at other times you might sit waiting for a return phone call. It might be that he or she is rejecting you or it might just be that the individual is at a different place on the S-curve from you. It might be that you need to pulse the relationship somewhat to energize it again or possibly redefine it because one of you has moved onto a different S-curve.

Figure 9.4   Network members' individual S-curves

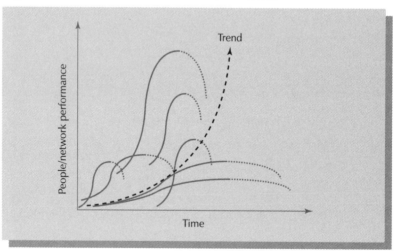

A common tragedy

One of the biggest potential problems with any network is abuse of the social capital fund. This is not the overt or predetermined decision to use more social capital than anyone else in the network. It is a subtle human dynamic where a stock of shared assets can be slowly depleted and eroded without anyone taking responsibility for the lessening.

This happens because of a problem known as the 'tragedy of the commons'. The 'commons' is any resource shared by a community of people. Such things as air, water and basic food come from commons. The tragedy that sits behind this is as follows. Consider a small village that is ably supported by a convenience store. The storeowner has an effective stock management process and keeps the shop well stocked so people can always pretty much get what they want. The store acts as a common resource that people in the village use to get their daily and weekly supplies as it saves them taking the 30-mile journey to the nearest large supermarket.

That is, until the fuel strike looms. As with all emergencies like this, panic can set in early. The thought of what might happen often exceeds the fact of what will happen. The first thing that people do on the Monday morning is to buy the daily bread, and get a spare one just in case. They also get some extra milk, just in case. As one person is walking home from the store, he mentions that he is topping up (just in case) to a neighbour, who in turn walks briskly to the store to top up (just in case). This trickle grows into a torrent until lunchtime when the store is stripped bare of bread, milk and other essentials. As a result, the storekeeper decides to make a quick visit to the wholesaler to top up (just in case), and so the myth and behaviour are perpetuated.

What was a common stock of assets has been depleted, not by any one person, but by a collective unconscious that erodes the resource. Each person just focuses on his or her little bit of improvement and sees that he/she can benefit without seeming to significantly diminish the amount of stock left for other people. Only once you helicopter above the individual perspective and see the system in its entirety can the enormity of the depletive process be observed. This type of behaviour can be seen time and time again in many situations: the depletion of fish stock as each trawler takes just a few more fish; the depletion of the oil reserves as each petroleum company seeks to get to the oil field before its competitor; the escalation of a small argument in a bar to a full-scale riot; or the small jar of peanuts in the centre of a table in the bar, as individuals struggle to clear the current mouthful so they can grab the last peanut!

> The tragedy of the commons lies in the failure to recognize that all people are attempting to do the same thing,

The problem with the tragedy of the commons lies in the failure to recognize that all people are attempting to do the same thing, but none sees the overall damage they are inflicting. Thus, on average, one unit of gain for each person produces a net one unit of cost for someone else. However, selfish people gain from the commons by acquiring more than their fair share of the resources and paying less than their fair share of the total costs. Ultimately, as population grows and greed runs rampant, the commons collapses and ends in 'the tragedy of the commons'.[26]

> Ultimately, as population grows and greed runs rampant, the common collapses and ends in tragedy.

Let us use the idea to understand how networks operate. If we use the S-curve model mentioned earlier, there will a point when the emerging network has a mass of social capital that acts as a central resource for the community to draw upon. People can call upon favours, use the network to bridge contacts, get clients in new domains, draw on others for emotional support, borrow a few ideas and so on, as seen in Figure 9.5. A manifestation of the abundance of social capital can be seen in the way that e-mail is managed within the community. Whenever e-mail is received from another member of the community, people will open it with interest to see what is going on and how they can help or get involved. All goes well until one person decides to take a big withdrawal. He sends an e-mail to the whole community that advertises his latest product. The great thing for that community member is that he has been able to actively market his new programme for virtually no cost. Now this is an interesting conundrum. Is he using the social capital of the network as a resource to help enhance his personal capital or is this blatant selling, something that might cross an invisible line in the sand, a line that is very important to many people in the network? Imagine that this network is built upon an unspoken principle that people are free to access each other, but only for support and sharing, not selling.

However, one of the members of the community receives the e-mail and recognizes that this is a powerful and cheap way to market her services. So she also decides to send out a blanket e-mail that promotes her latest product. Now the idea gets momentum and within a week up to 50% of the network members are actively using the network as a 'market' rather than a 'channel to market'.

The result of this shared behaviour by a large group of people within the network means that people don't open e-mails from the network any more because all they expect is a sales pitch. As a result, they are starting to migrate from the community and look elsewhere for support. Conversely, the people sending the e-mails keep getting failed receipts on their system and so assume that the person no longer wants to be in the network and deletes the person from the distribution list. The tragedy is that no one person has not

Figure 9.5 Social capital as a common resource

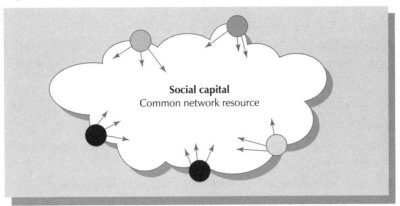

depleted the common area of social capital, rather the collective unconscious has contributed to the collapse of the common area as each person has taken his or her little piece of the common resource, as seen in Figure 9.6.

Now this assumes that the unspoken behaviour is driven by the idea that people are not aware of the fact that they are destroying these common resources. However, the bigger problem is when people are very conscious that there is a limited resource that is about to be depleted. As a result, they set out on a campaign of deliberate destruction of the commons to not only get the wealth out of it before someone else does, but also to leave nothing

Figure 9.6 Social capital common area erosion

PERSONAL NETWORKING

for others. Think about the wanton physical destruction that often can be left after mankind searches for rare assets (Amazon rainforest being one example). This is simply a process of personal greed focused on the accumulation of all the assets held with the common pool before someone else can acquire them. From a networking perspective, these might be called the networking mongrels, people who just use and abuse networks.[27] They might:

- collect business cards and fake social interest without any intention to follow up on the meeting;
- try to make a sale at weddings, a birthday party or some other social engagement;
- focus on what they want rather than fostering the collective abundance;
- be driven by quantity rather than quality.

The challenge as a member of the network (assuming that because it is a community you cannot mandate fixes) is to see what you can do to prevent this tragedy from occurring. There is clearly no simple answer to what is a deep human condition, but there are a few suggestions that might help to ease the pain:[28]

> The challenge as a member of the network (assuming that because it is a community you cannot mandate fixes) is to see what you can do to prevent this tragedy from occurring.

- If you believe that the common social capital is being depleted, be brave and tell people. If you get e-mails that offend you or go against the network ethos, then tell people. Maybe circulate a discussion document or set up a chat page on your website.

- Maybe try to replenish the common area by introducing new people to the network. Ensure that they are 'net-givers' and will not enter the network purely to take from what they see as a full resource pool.

- Remove the constraints that limit the resource pool. Maybe cross-pollinate your network with other networks. Become a boundary spanner so that you can find resource in other communities that you can import in the area being depleted.

- If you are really finding it difficult to stem the depletion, then maybe suggest to the network that it self-imposes certain rules and guidelines for operation. This happens on many Web discussion groups where people are restricted to the number of words they can use in a note or there is agreement over the use of bad language.

■ Set a personal example. Take a soapbox position that you are conscious of certain problems or issues and you intend to change your personal behaviour. Don't overtly suggest that anyone else should change, but by taking a leadership position there is a chance that others will value your intervention and follow.

Manage the memes

Genes exist in the human body to control the inheritance of specific physical characteristics and are made up of deoxyribonucleic acid (DNA). In the same way, organizations can be viewed as having memes. These are the units of cultural transmission, or packets of ideas and knowledge that are used to spread information through the network. The evolutionary biologist Richard Dawkins in his book *The Selfish Gene* originated this word. He suggests that memes are contagious information patterns that are copied inside a community or group of individuals. They are passed from mind to mind through human interaction, and shape how the network thinks, feels and behaves.

The difference between an idea and a meme is that an idea is passive, whereas a meme might be seen to have a life of its own. It will be seen almost as a living force that evolves and adapts as it spreads through an organization. These can be commonly seen in the propagation of catchphrases, pop tunes, inventions and fashions that develop in social systems. Importantly, one person's idea for a catchphrase or song is not a meme. The meme only comes in to being when it is repeated to someone else, and hence becomes transmitted knowledge or information. An example might be if the reader of this book goes to another person, and tells him about the idea of a meme: the theory of the meme is then in itself a meme within that social system.

> Memes are the units of cultural transmission, or packets of ideas and knowledge that are used to spread information through the network.

In many ways, a meme has the characteristic of a virus, but instead it is information or knowledge that is passed from one person to another, both consciously and unconsciously. Once created, a virus of the mind gains a life independent of its creator, and evolves quickly to infect as many people as possible. A strong meme that is repeatedly shared can be found to spread quickly through an organization. A weak meme does not gain acceptance and so rapidly dies.

An example of a network meme might be the rumour that someone in the network is about to set up a business. This will often take a life of its own, and can be dispersed around the organization in days, or in some cases minutes. Now, at this stage, the thought has a life of its own. It might die out, as people realize that it is false information. Alternatively, it might hang around in people's subconscious, and start to influence and infect decisions they take. The characteristics of a meme can be summarized as follows:

- They generally contain bait. This is the personal payback that the individual gets for receiving and passing on the information.
- Memes are stored in the belief space, and this can only accept so many. Once full, memes have to compete to hold on to the space.
- They contain a hook, which is the part of the idea that encourages replication.
- They can change as they are replicated and so the ideas and stories can be seen to drift over time.

What does all this mean to the idea of network socialization? In essence, in the same way that people are critically aware of the damaging impact that software viruses can have on their operational performance, networks must also be acutely aware of the impact of memes on the way that knowledge is transferred across the community and how it affects the choice-making processes.

People should be encouraged to be aware of the content of their belief space and, in particular, the source of the beliefs. They should be able to differentiate between memes that are valid and of value, and those that are inaccurate or malicious. The organization should also be aware of any dubious memes that are living within the business, and the damage that they might be doing to the knowledge creation process.

As an example, people in the network can be encouraged to consider things they hear from network members and then consider where the idea actually came from, how valid it is, how they know it is true and who they shared the ideas with. If they are unable to answer these questions clearly, then how can they be sure that they have not been infected with a meme that is false or counterfeit, and even more, to what extent they have acted as a host for the meme to replicate itself onto other people?

Although the idea of meme management can be seen as woolly, the meme is a significant factor that can seriously damage a social community if let loose. The impact of spurious and false rumours can damage the growth of the network in the following ways:

- **Trust** – what chance will you have of building think-trust relationships if people have heard negative things about you?

- **Shadows** – once the memes enter the shadow area and are not discussed in your presence, what chance will you have to counteract or put right the false messages?

- **Personal promotion** – if the rumours abound and sit in the shadow, then any time you try to present an image to the network people might listen politely but internally overlay your comments with the 'truths' they have heard about you.

The important thing with negative memes is to understand just how damaging they can be when unchecked in a social network and to consider what steps you can take to effect some degree of regulation. There are no simple answers to managing memes, but one primary action is often around surfacing the meme the moment you become conscious of its existence. You can rarely fix a rumour that is not surfaced; only once the issue can be discussed will it be possible to get from fantasy and back to the facts.

Organization and disorganization

Many organizations are based on mechanistic or machine-based operating principles. Consider the typical assumptions that drive the formation of an organization's management system. The first supposition is that equilibrium, stability, and control are the desired states. The next is that organizations can be separated into discrete components (function, department, product groups, etc.), and these elements can operate independently of any other unit within the business. Third, organizations should always allocate resources in trying to determine what the market will look like in one, three and five years' time; and that cause and effect relationships can be traced through the business and that when something goes wrong in one part of the business it can be isolated and repaired without affecting other areas.[29]

The assumptions are driven by a set of deep underlying ideas:

- *'We can know the future'*. Organizations are often awash with market forecasters, business planners, strategy builders and economists who advise the organization of what is likely to happen in the future. The whole premise, on which these positions exist, is that the future can be predicted and managed.

- *'Divide and conquer'*. There is often a desire to divide the organization into management chunks on the assumption that things can be taken apart, dissected and split asunder (as with business functions and academic disciplines). The conjecture is that by comprehending the workings of each piece, the whole can be managed.[30] The chunking that might typically be seen in organizations is by function (marketing, engineering, finance, etc.), geography, hierarchy, product groups or project teams.

- **'Let me tell you what is wrong'**. Most systems operate on negative feedback. Control systems – such as objective setting, budgetary structures, and resource allocations – are driven by a common approach. People are asked to forecast what is required, report any variance against the forecast, and then take action to rectify and limit the variance.

- **'The boss knows best'**. This can be best summed up as the manager knows best. The common structural map is that the people at the top know best and only need to draw upon the views of the lower teams to pick up a few tit-bits and give them a pat on the head.

- **'Don't feel – think'**. Organizations are typically (overtly) driven by tasks, business goals, corporate objectives and the assumptions that people come to work for the love of the business. Often there is a view that people's feelings are left at home. Many organizations can be built around the idea of a repressed model, where any mention of emotion or sentiment in a business meeting can be enough to cause an apoplexy for the traditional manager. The base (espoused) assumption is that business decisions are based on logic and sensible decision-making processes. The reality is that they are often driven by personal ambition, greed and fear as much as for the good of the business.

> With the self-organization model, the emphasis is placed more upon the nature of connectivity within the system, namely, the interconnections, the configuration and the map of the relationship between the components as well as the role of the people.

However, there is little chance that a fully functional professional network could ever operate on such constructs. Should you even attempt to tie a group of network agents together in such a fashion it would probably kill the community at birth.

Instead the network has to be founded upon an entirely different set of operating principles. It has to be founded around the idea of a community that can spontaneously self-organize itself and adapt to changing market conditions. This can be seen as the ability of a group of people to unexpectedly manage themselves without any intervention or control from an external agent. Self-organization demands that a system draw upon its own resources, not the hierarchy's, in order to meet the challenges that it faces.[31] Like birds flocking in the sky, children in the playground, people leaving a football stadium, or massed peace rallies, once the boundaries are set, and simple rules are offered, then harmony can emerge from a situation that is apparently chaotic, essentially 'order for free'.[32]

One of the significant factors with the mechanistic organization is that emphasis is placed upon the cogs in the system. This means that people have defined roles, objectives, and their place in a robust hierarchy. With the self-organization model, the emphasis is placed more upon the nature of connectivity within the system, namely, the interconnections, the configuration and the map of the relationship between the components as well as the role of the people.

Effective networks will exhibit the following characteristics:

- **Self-stability**. There is a high degree of stability, not in the traditional sense of being fixed or unvarying, but in the capability to maintain the same overall structure in spite of any changes or replacement of component parts. The nature of the system means that it is able to remain steady, even when small disturbances occur. Since the inherent design of the system is based upon adaptability and self-regulation, it is able to contain any surprises which might occur that could be disruptive. If the people in the network want to be in the network, then it will survive. It will change and adapt every day, week and month, but it will survive.

- **Self-reproducing**. This suggests that the network can continually reproduce itself in order to meet its goals in two ways. First, while the overall structure of the community remains the same, the components or people in the network will continually change. In doing this, it modifies its internal elements but retains its overall identity. An example of this can be seen in the way that people rebuild their pancreas every 24 hours, the stomach lining every three days, and blood every month. The body is able to do this because it continually regenerates and changes the cell structure within the body.[33]

- **Self-regulation**. Underpinning this idea of the self-sustaining organization is the notion of intrinsic self-regulation. Intrinsic regulation is where the network has its own capacity to regulate its operation and hence its output. Extrinsic regulation is where the control comes from outside the natural system. Networks will typically be intrinsically managed because no one person has the right to say what is and isn't right or wrong.

■ **Self-organizing**. Natural organisms can have a tendency to be attracted to an instinctive style or pattern of working. This natural or stable state is often known as the attractor state, a way of operating where order naturally arises out of disorder. For example, look at a group of school children playing at lunchtime. There is apparent disorder and chaos, but if the picture is considered in terms of patterns and relationships, different shapes and behavioural patterns will emerge. It will be possible to see patterns in the guise of repeated games that instigate a set of behaviours. Football will set up one pattern while the game of '*it*' will drive another pattern. Networks will intuitively set up self-regulated patterns that form around a common point of interest. If you can understand the nature of the attractor, then you will start to understand the nature of the network and how it self-organizes.

The key message about self-organizing systems is that as people migrate from a mechanistic or organized system to operate in an open network, they might need to lose some of the beliefs in the gods of direction, stability, and consistency. Networks are very rarely like this.

Knowledge socialization

The introduction of new knowledge into a network community can be aligned directly to the idea of launching a new product. As ideas diffuse through a social network it is socialized, accepted and further diffused by the people in the internal market in the same way that a product will enter a new market.

The diffusion process might be considered as the social change that occurs as the idea is accepted within the community. Since the rate at which different people adopt a new idea will vary, it is possible to develop distinct categories that indicate the stages of diffusion. These types represent the degree to which people are innovative. Are they prepared to accept and work with change and new ideas or do they prefer to wait for the idea to become established and part of the mainstream before they will socialize it? This innovative nature is not just an attitudinal acceptance of the new idea, but a positive behavioural step change that indicates an individual's willingness to modify his or her schematic framework. The willingness to accept new ideas by individuals in the organization can be mapped against time and the resulting profile can be constructed to indicate the total rate of diffusion across the business.

There are five classic types of people who play a role in the socialization of knowledge within a network:

- innovators
- early adopters
- early majority
- late majority
- laggards.

These categories can be mapped against a standard deviation curve in order to understand the percentage of types that can be found in typical organizations (Figure 9.7).[34]

Figure 9.7 Standard deviations of innovators, early adopters, early majority, late majority, laggards

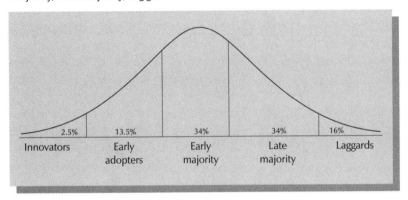

| 2.5% | 13.5% | 34% | 34% | 16% |
| Innovators | Early adopters | Early majority | Late majority | Laggards |

- **Innovators**. These people are venturesome in that they are happy to move beyond the ideas of their peer group to try new ideas and experiences. They have a tendency to do things that are rash and exciting, and have a disposition to act as the entry point, or for new ideas to enter into their social group.
- **Early adopters**. These people act as missionaries for change, helping to lead the change and diffusion process through the organization. They are adventurous enough to take risks, but have enough influence in the critical mass groups to help to facilitate change across the business.
- **Early majority**. They welcome new ideas shortly before the average people in the organization. They are in a position where they interact regularly with their peers but are not normally opinion formers within the business. They take their time before adopting a new framework, possibly because they take longer to make the decision to accept the change.

- **Late majority**. This group accepts the idea after the average members in the organization, but will be sceptical about new ideas and will possibly accept the change only after peer pressure forces acceptance of the innovation.

- **Laggards**. This is the last group in the organization to accept a new idea or piece of knowledge. They will take decisions based on historic reasoning rather than consider what is right for today or tomorrow. It is important to understand that their resistance to new ideas is undertaken as a standpoint that is entirely rational from their viewpoint.

Although many conclusions might be drawn about this categorization, a key one is that the essence of effective knowledge diffusion through a network is driven by peer imitation. In deciding whether to internalize a new idea, people will be heavily influenced by their companions, and especially those who are in the higher adoption category. Hence, this might indicate the power that dominant opinion leaders within the network can have upon the acceptance of a new idea. As such, any network agent should have an appreciation of this power if he/she is to be effective in the networker role. Conversely, the community should be acutely aware of the location of these opinion formers and understand the potential that they have to amplify or attenuate ideas and knowledge. Consider the implication of a person who falls into the late majority or laggard category and sits in a gatekeeper position within the network.

> One of the ways in which the blockage presented by a passive gatekeeper can be overcome is through the generation of sufficient critical mass. The critical mass is the point where enough people have accepted the new idea that further adoption becomes self-sustaining.

This might be someone who has strong ties with a lot of the community or maybe someone who is a weak tie and acts as a bridge to another network. Wherever the gatekeeper sits, if his/her criteria and rationale for taking decisions are driven by playing safe and taking a more traditional view of life, then he or she can act as a blocker. What happens then if the network wants to acquire new knowledge about an emerging topic area that this person has access to? In effect, the entire learning process can be slowed down or stalled because a few people are able to block the flow process. This scenario gets worse the more powerful the individual is within the network. Although the irony is that if the gatekeeper is on your side and acts as a

Figure 9.8 The significance of the gatekeeper

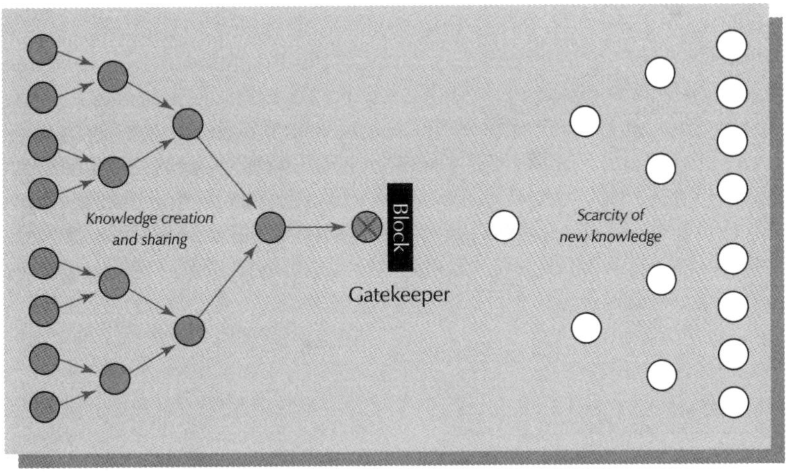

sponsor, then he/she increases your return on investment by opening doors for you, but the risk is that if one word is out of place, you are blocked and prevented from gaining access to the area that you might most need.[35]

One of the ways in which the blockage presented by a passive gatekeeper can be overcome is through the generation of sufficient critical mass. The critical mass is the point where enough people have accepted the new idea that further adoption becomes self-sustaining. Like a ball bouncing in a room full of mouse traps, a stage is reached where the released mouse traps start to bounce around and end up setting off further traps. At this stage the room is into the idea of positive feedback, and the process will continue irrespective of any impact the ball is making.

The crucial idea in sharing knowledge across the network is to identify those connections whose adoption will most rapidly influence other people to join in the sharing process. Rogers[12] suggests some possible strategies that might be used to develop critical mass around an idea that is being shared[36]:

■ Target key people for the initial adoption of a new idea or knowledge. Adoption by this group will send the appropriate signal to people that the idea is desirable.

■ Create a positive aura around the idea by implying that the end result is inevitable and that the market will accept it.

■ Introduce the idea to network subgroups where there is a good chance that the members are likely to adopt the idea at once. Taking a whole group at one time increases the ability to reach critical mass early on in the diffusion process.

■ Provide incentives for the early adoption of the idea until critical mass is achieved.

Although creating critical mass is important in the diffusion of knowledge or ideas with a network, in overly focusing on this there is a danger that the sharing process can shift from a collaborative and open style to one that is manipulative and hidden. This will ultimately be counter-productive to the underlying principles that drive the desire to create a learning environment. The goal is to understand the idea of critical mass and how it affects the diffusion process; it is not to encourage the entire population to play games to get their ideas researched.

In summary

Ask yourself:

■ To what extent do I seek to manage those factors that will cause my network to decay?

■ To what extent do I actively seek to correct instances where the social capital is being abused by the network?

■ To what extent do I seek to minimize erroneous distortions that flow around the network?

■ To what extent do I maintain a balance between the loose and tight network management processes?

■ To what extent do I understand the various gates and amplifiers that help ideas to flow through the network?

Network management

So there you have it – the Personal Networking Framework. The suggestion is that if you are able to take some time out to consider and manage a number of areas considered in this model, then your ability to make personal connections count will be enhanced. Management of these six areas will not guarantee wealth, health and happiness, but in my experience they will contribute to the growth of your social capital, which in turn puts you in a much stronger position in the world.

Part of the ability to make sure that your social capital does add value will be dependent upon the extent to which you consciously take time to monitor and manage the state of your network. A key ingredient in this process will be to use the network connection chart (Figure 10.1) as a diagnostic tool

Figure 10.1   Network connection chart

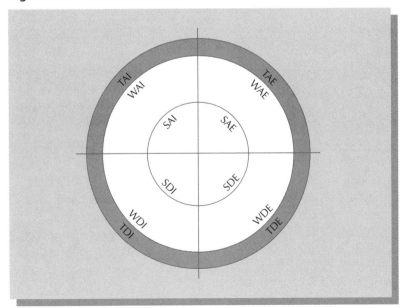

or instrument that will allow you to highlight certain characteristics that might need to be tuned or acted upon. Some of the features you might observe and ask questions about include:

- **Network density**. Do you have a configuration that is over-dense? To what extent do the people in your network have a relationship with each other and does this mean that little fresh air is being used to refresh and invigorate the network?

- **Network bias**. To what extent is there a bias in your connection towards a particular type of person? Do you have a concentration in one area? For example, do you favour strong ties over weak; alike over different relationships; or extrinsic over intrinsic? Maybe the bias works for you at present but will it hold up in the future?

> This book and model are about professional networking and not developing a network of friends. Sometimes you have to say the party is over; however, the ethical way is to do this openly and honestly. The worst thing in the world is to close a tie down and not tell the person.

- **New connections**. To what extent do you have new contacts targeted and what type of connection do you need them to be? Are the new connections the right ones, taking into account the current chart biases and construction?

- **Redundant connections**. To what extent do you need to selectively move strong ties into weak ties and weak ties out of the network domain? Far too often people hold on to network relationships for historic reasons rather than for the value added contribution. I know this is a contentious point because you don't like to feel like you are dumping people, but this book and model are about professional networking and not developing a network of friends. Sometimes you have to say the party is over; however, the ethical way is to do this openly and honestly. The worst thing in the world is to close a tie down and not tell the person.

- **Strong tie clusters**. Is there a dominance of strong ties within the network? If you have predominantly strong ties, does this give you enough boundary spanners to ensure that you can touch other networks? Might your network be viewed as a dense interconnecting group of people or can it be viewed as an open system with links that splay off over the horizon?

- **Weak ties**. To what extent is your network linked or related to other networks through bridging agents? What are these networks and if you need to grow links with them can you engineer further boundary spanners to bridge the relationship? How locked in are you to any key weak ties that help you bridge other networks? What is the impact on your personal capital if you lose contact with these people?

- **Intrinsic/extrinsic clusters**. Have you built your network around the people or the function they perform? If around the intrinsic person, do you have sufficient access to the role that people perform? Or if around extrinsic factors, do you have back-up contacts for when those people change job and move on into new roles? Look for cross-matches with other factors. For example, do you have a high cluster of SAE people (strong, alike and extrinsic)? This would suggest that you are spending a lot of time with a close group of people who all share a similar interest. If your personal goal is to diversify in readiness for a career move, does this really help bridge into the areas you want to move into?

- **Abundance levels**. When you chart the level of abundance established with each person, is there a prominent trend? Have you built a large network with a spread of diverse and rich contacts but very little abundance? Do you have buckets of contacts but find that you are in a subordinate role with many of them? Do you have a cluster of strong ties but you are actually getting more from them than they are getting from you and will end up with a bad brand?

- **Shadow forces**. As you look across the network, is there a sense of open and honest debate where people are not frightened to talk about traditionally taboo subjects or do you sense a degree of protective language where certain subjects or people are not surfaced? Where shadows do exist, do they have the potential to sabotage the network and cause it to collapse amidst rancour and acrimony or are they acceptable and any effort to surface and resolve them might end up causing more trouble?

- **Differentiation factors**. How differentiated is your network? Do you associate with people who are able to clearly stand out from the crowd or have you grouped with people who position themselves at a commodity level? How do they perceive you and your brand – are you suitably differentiated?

> A key ingredient in this process will be to use the network connection chart as a diagnostic tool or instrument that will allow you to highlight certain characteristics that might need to be tuned or acted upon.

■ **Brand wrap**. Although it can be difficult to quantify, it can be important to understand if your network is perceived as the place to be! Do you have people calling to find out about making contact with you and your colleagues or do you have to initiate calls? If your network creates a pull in the market, then this suggests that it has some brand strength; if however the converse is true, then maybe the brand is not that prominent. There is no right level of brand prominence, as some networks will want to be very conspicuous whereas others will prefer to sit in the background. The important thing is to understand the gap between where you think it needs to be and where it is.

> There is no right level of brand prominence, as some networks will want to be very conspicuous whereas others will prefer to sit in the background. The important thing is to understand the gap between where you think it needs to be and where it is.

■ **Trust fund statement**. If you were to run an end-of-year review, what would the trust fund statement look like? Is the network accumulating credit and does it show an overall credit, or is it beginning to show that debits are accumulating within the community? If averaged out, would it show a net deficit within the balance of internal payments and if so what actions could you take to rectify the problem. The trouble is that negative trust funds may not cause problems today but they will almost always act as a potential issue for the future. No sustainable and ethical network can really survive and prosper for long without trust. The trick is to constantly monitor the level of confidence across the networks and take action before it creates problems.

■ **Meme flows**. How do memes flow around the network? Do ideas and thoughts get picked up and transported across the network with ease or are there blockages that cause the memes to stop in their tracks at certain junctures? What memes are adding value to the network members? What memes are not adding value and how can you act to ensure that the negative members do not end up driving shadows within the community?

■ **Rate of knowledge emergence**. Does new knowledge emerge from within the network or does it have to be imported? The ability to create and manage knowledge within the network can offer a huge commercial advantage to the members, where the need to import knowledge can result in a high level of market taxation as people need to buy books, places on courses and seats at conferences just to find out what is happening. The ability to create knowledge within the network also ensures that members are ahead of the market and can be seen as pathfinders and representatives of their particular domain.

> It can be interesting to undertake a temporal analysis of your network and map the changes that have occurred in two-month blocks.

- **Flow position**. Where on the S-curve would you place the whole network? Is it in the emergent, strong, mature or declining phase of its lifecycle? Do you need to make any investment to help push it up the S-curve? Where are the various key people in the network on this curve? Do you have some key people who have weak ties, extrinsic value and dissimilar interests and, if so, where are they on the curve? What impact will it have if they opt out of the network?

- **Time shift**. One of the important things about networking is that it often happens in the background. So much of it is based upon casual contacts, passing e-mails and drop-in sessions that our network structure can shift almost imperceptibly over time. It can be interesting to undertake a temporal analysis of your network and map the changes that have occurred in two-month blocks. Who have you met? Who did you discard? How have relationships shifted? Much of what you see will be known, but you might also start to see unconscious patterns that were not so obvious. For example, I meet many people who say that they want to leave their current job and start their own business, but when challenged on their networking activity, most of the growth areas have been with other people within the company rather than with WDE (weak, different, extrinsic) ties that could help them make the step into a new career.

The questions raised above can only really skim the surface of the factors that help a professional network to function effectively. The purpose of the network connection chart is to give you some of the forces that impact on the generation and flow of social capital. The next step is for you to spend serious time working through and understanding these forces in more depth and then using them to map your past, present and projected network.

The network connection chart is not a panacea for the development of a professional network. What it will do is offer a simple but powerful framework that will help you make the choices that are necessary to the generation of high-value social capital. The whole process of making the right social choices can be a vexing and stressful one. However, by using the network connection chart you can feel more confident that the choices you make are correct and will add to the long-term process of turning personal capital into social capital.

Finally, the creation of social capital is a natural human trait. The trouble is that it is not taught at school, is rarely considered at college, and only occasionally introduced as a formal training topic at work. However, all through life's stages it is something that we do as naturally as breathing. The goal of this book is to suggest that maybe it is time to understand how you currently create value and really start to think about how you can improve this process for the betterment of yourself, your colleagues and society in general.

Epilogue

As Leo Borwick, a colleague in my network, pointed out:

> It is well known that if you put a load of antique dealers on a desert island, they will proceed to sell each other the same pieces of junk round and round at ever increasing prices until they are all rich and living comfortably.

The whole point of building a network is to amplify your personal capital. Be careful that you always network with a purpose and do not spend all your time and energy building a wonderful network that is loved by all its members but which offers little real value outside the group.

All the best – good luck on your journey and let me know how you get on at mick@wizoz.co.uk

Mick
www.wizoz.co.uk

Notes

1. Baker, Wayne (2000) *Achieving Success through Social Capital*. San Francisco: Jossey Bass, p. 1.
2. Coen and Prusak, *In Good Company, How Social Capital Makes Organisations Work*. Boston: Harvard Business School Press, p. 16.
3. Bacon, Kevin, *The Small-World, and Why It All Matters*. (http://www.santafe.edu/sfi/publications/Bulletins/bulletinFall99/workIn Progress/smallWorld.html) Vol. 14, No. 2.
4. For more on the step inside-out principle, see Cope, Mick (2002) *Lead Yourself*. London: Pearson.
5. Egan, (1994) *Working the Shadow Side*. Josey Bass, p. 35.
6. Cialdini, Robert (1984) *The Psychlogy of Influence*. Quill, an imprint of William Morrow and Company Inc.
7. Granovetter, Mark (1974) *Getting a Job; A study on Contacts and Careers*. Cambridge, MA; Harvard University Press.
8. Gittel, Ross and Vidal, Avid (1998) *Community Organizing*. London: Sage Publications, p. 19.
9. Irving, Janis (1972) *Victims of Groupthink*. Boston: Houghton Mifflin; Irving, Janis (1982) *Groupthink: Psychological Studies of Policy Decisions and Fiascos*. 2nd edn. Boston: Houghton Mifflin.
10. Putnam, Robert D. (2000) *Bowling Alone*. New York: Touchstone, Simon and Schuster, p. 352.
11. Peters, Tom (1999) *Brand You 50*. Borzoi Books, Alfred A. Knopf Inc., p. 111.
12. Handy, Charles (2001), *The Elephant and the Flea*. London: Hutchinson, p. 32.
13. Peters, Tom, *Brand You 50*, Borzoi books, Published by Alfred A Knopf Inc, 1999, p. 102.
14. For more on personal capital see Cope, Mick (2000) *Know your Value? – Value What You Know*. London: Pearson.
15. http://www.thephilosophyclinic.com/OntoMarket.html – 27 July 2002.
16. Webbe, Alan M. *Fast Company*, Issue 38 p. 210 http://www.fastcompany.com/online/38/roberts.html.

17. Reback, Jerome, *Be Yourself, Not the Brand*
    http://www.smythedorward.com/epreview/epreview_may02.htm
18. http://www.dictionary.com.
19. BBC Reith Lectures 2002 – 'A Question of Trust'.
20. Fukuyama, Francis, (1996) *Trust*. London: Harper Collins.
21. Grant, John (1999) *The New Marketing Manifesto*. Orion Business,
    p. 111.
22. Mulgan, Geoff (1998) *Connexity*, London: Pub Vintage, p. 100.
23. *Ibid.*, p. 160.
24. Cialdini, Robert B. (1993) *The Psychology of Persuasion*. William
    Morrow.
25. Sullivan, Nancy, *Highlands Culture*
    http://www.altnews.com.au/jetsunstudios/travelcam/highcul.htm
26. Hardin, Garrett (1968) *Science* 162:1243.
27. Vilas, Sandy and Fisher, Dona (1996) *The Power of Networking*.
    London: Thorsons, p. 9.
28. Senge, Peter, *et al.*, (1994) *The Fifth Discipline Field Book*. London:
    Nicholas Brealey.
29. For more on this, see Cope, Mick (1998) *Leading the Organisation to
    Learn*. London: Pearson.
30. Wheatley, Margaret (1994) *Leadership and the New Science*.
31. Goldstein, Jeffrey (1994) *The Unshackled Organisation*. Norman
    Bodek, p. 3.
32. Kaufmann, Stuart (1995) *Order for Free*. Penguin Books, p. 71.
33. Capra, Fritof (1997) *The Web of Life*, Harper Collins, p. 213.
34. Everett, Rogers (1995) *Diffusion of Innovations*, 4th ed, The Free
    Press, p. 317.
35. Locket, Jon (1999) *Powerful Networking.* London: Orion Business
    Books, p. 45.
36. Everett, Rogers (1995) Diffusion of Innovations, 4 edn. The Free
    Press, p. 317.

Appendix

Network frame

Activate abundance

1. **Self-abundance** – I have confidence in my personal value.
2. **Sow before you reap** – I invest in relationships with others without expecting anything in return.
3. **Level of abundance** – I always seek to create a shared success with others and avoid selfish routines.
4. **Love the one you're with** – I have strategies that allow me to resolve the issue of networking with people I don't like.
5. **Slingshot – use your net's net** – I know what other networks my colleagues are members of.

Build bridges

6. **See their world** – I attempt to modify my behaviour and language to help others feel comfortable.
7. **Knowing you – selling me** – I have a personal promotion strategy.
8. **See the shadows** – I have strategies to help surface the shadow issues with others.
9. **Listen to the language** – I seek to manage language to stimulate a compound conversation.
10. **Be likeable** – I try to help other people to like me.

Chart the connections

11. **Tie strength** – I have the optimum balance of strong and weak ties in my network.

12. **Similarity** – I have the optimum mix of similar and dissimilar people in my network.
13. **Relational value** – I have the optimum mix of intrinsic and extrinsic value people in my network.
14. **Network connection chart** – I have a clear view of the biases within my network structure.
15. **Network abundance** – I am clear as to the value potential with each of my network connections.

Dare to be different

16. **You and you alone** - I am clear as to my personal unique selling point.
17. **Bang the symbol** – I can represent who I am or what I do in a memorable symbol or phrase.
18. **Find it – don't fake it** – I am always authentic in my relationships.
19. **Simply simple** – I can offer a simple statement that sums up my value to the network.
20. **Sell yourself** – I can do a 60-second pitch to promote my value to a colleague.

Entrust others

21. **Pressing the flesh** – I always seek to manage trust
22. **Trust choice** – I understand the factors that impact upon my choice to trust someone.
23. **Trust funds** – I can describe the level of my trust fund with each network connection.
24. **Transferable trust** – I am conscious of when I transfer trust within the network.
25. **Give to get** – I am conscious of the reciprocity transactions that occur with my connections.

Fuel the flow

26. **Ride the S-curve** – I seek to manage those factors that will cause my network to decay.
27. **A common tragedy** – I actively seek to correct instances where the social capital is being abused by the network.

28. **Manage the memes** – I seek to minimize erroneous distortions that flow around the network.
29. **Organization and disorganization** – I maintain a balance between the loose and tight network management processes.
30. **Knowledge socialization** – I understand the various gates and amplifiers that help ideas to flow through the network.

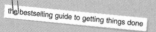
the bestselling guide to getting things done

Simply
Brilliant

SIMPLY BRILLIANT
The competitive advantage of common sense
Fergus O'Connell

ISBN 0 273 65418 7

"Simply Brilliant is brilliantly simple – so much so that I might start coming to work to get things done." *Financial Times*

"Tears down management as a complex science, reducing it to life saving basics. This book does a good job – it may just help to simplify your working life" *Evening Standard*

"O'Connell's ideas for creating a better working environment are as simple as he claims and will provide welcome relief for anyone who is struggling to come to terms with the latest fad from the Harvard Business School…" *The Sunday Times*

Life is complicated enough. Yet many people go out of their way to create hoops to jump through, wrestling with tough problems and calling on the latest management fad to find that elusive solution to a problem. But it doesn't have to be that way. The best ideas aren't always complicated. The world is full of smart, experienced, skilled, brilliant people. However, many people – even smart ones – are lacking a set of essential skills that when pulled together can be termed 'common sense'. Shortlisted for the WHS Business Book of the Year 2002 and a runaway international bestseller, *Simply Brilliant* features a set of seven principles to make the bright better. Principles of common sense that can be adapted for attacking many of the problems that you encounter every day, be it in work or outside.

Simply Brilliant – you'll be amazed at the difference it can make.

Visit our website at
www.business-minds.com